Hang on to Your Stars

The First 90 Days: A Step-by-Step Employee
Engagement Solution for the Senior Living
Community

Doreen A. Lang

First Printing, 2017

ISBN 978-0-692-93857-7

HANG ON TO YOUR STARS LLC

www.hangontoyourstars.com

What Others Are Saying

"As an RN with more than forty-five years of management experience in both the private sector as well as direct care, I felt my knowledge of recruitment and staff retention was fairly solid. However, after reading Doreen Lang's new book I found gems of wisdom on every page. This is a MUST-read for anyone who manages a staff in eldercare or in any industry."

— Jean E. Niece RN, Administrator, Sartwell Place Assisted Living at The Morrison

"Doreen's book defines how to plan for success instead of failure! She explains how to build commitment amongst employees. Doreen helps managers see what is lost when staff turnover takes away good employees. Not only is there a financial toll on your business, but you lose the time you invested in those employees, their talents and expertise; – and maybe worst of all, – when you have high turnover, you are left with low morale amongst your remaining employees.

The engagement strategies in this book are innovative, simple, and practical and build from an employee's first day through what is hopefully years of dedication and hard work from talented and committed employees. Doreen gives managers the tools and strategies they can follow—and a big budget is not required! Just a willingness to invest in those people you want to invest in you and your business. An interesting and easy read, it –it will be great to have my department heads read the book and apply the principles.

READ this book—— it will inspire you to self-reflect on your management style and grow as a leader."

— Lara Shook, CEO/Executive Director at Peterborough
Independent Living

"Simply written, yet totally enlightening, this guide finally contains the answers to one of healthcare's biggest issues...how to keep your best employees. Doreen has not only done the research, but she has lived it. *Hang on to Your Stars* should be considered the bible for all managers in the healthcare industry."

— Mary E. Joyce, Former Activities Director
in Senior Living

"I love Doreen's writing style. She is a born teacher, motivator, and collaborator. I think her ideas are so very, very important for the business world to embrace."

— Carol Centrella, Retired Mental Health Worker,
McLean Hospital

Acknowledgements

Thank you to all my students and staff at the Boston area hospitals, The Dartmouth Group, Peabody Properties, The Pyramid Companies, The Welch Company and Hometown America for teaching me every day what it means to be engaged, thereby making me the best leader I can be.

A special thanks to my editor, MJ Plaster, the best editor on the planet. Thank you for your guidance, expertise, and professionalism. Without you, the readers would be so confused! When I met you, the stars must have been aligned. Because of your brightness, you make me shine. Thank you for your sense of humor and support when I needed it. You are one in a million.

Thank you, Ryan Travis, for your help in publishing my first book. You are a sterling example of why Boomers need to believe in Millennials. Thank you, Liz Dow—you did an outstanding job on the cover. You took my raw and unskilled pencil drawing and nailed it—such talent. Marie Fricker, a fabulous author and my own personal editorial consultant, your objective interpretation and feedback was a godsend. Olivia Miller, another fabulous author and expert editor, thank you for your expertise and the speed in which you helped us get this done. And special thanks to BeBe Watson, who provided great feedback and believes in this mission as much as I do.

Thank you to my very dear friend, Donna Stahl, who spent over 20+ years tirelessly working as a sales associate, only to receive a pink slip with a mumbled, "Sorry, but we are going in a different direction." On her way home from work that day, she called me and said, "Doreen, there is no heart in business." I will always think of her painful words that made such an impact on me. Thank you, Donna. I will continue to keep my heart in the work I do and how I want to inspire that in others.

Thank you to all my friends and to the many Millennials who responded to my survey questions. Thank you for helping me to learn from you.

And a heartfelt thank-you to my husband, Walter, who always believes in me, and to my children, Travis and Grace. Gracie, I hope to be as good a writer as you one day. Thank you for all your help in reviewing, editing, and proofing. You are outstanding.

Love you all, D

Contents

Author's Note

Early in my career, I was extremely dissatisfied and completely disillusioned with my work at a senior living community. The managers worked in silos; we weren't part of any shared vision, the leader was mostly absent, and I had no idea of how the community was doing financially. I felt disconnected and devalued. The organization also had a huge problem with employee retention. In my current role, I could only affect my small staff but did so with a high percent retention success because I had learned how to hang on to my stars. I did lose an employee who felt so inspired from the work she did with me that she left to start her own company. Sometimes no matter how much you "luv 'em," they leave.

The engagement process I had practiced with my staff created strong, loyal, and happy teams, but it was painful to see the lack of motivation and the absenteeism displayed by the other departments staff. In senior living, when the staff *is not engaged* and therefore lacks positive attitudes and commitment to excellence, the residents suffer. I was frustrated and upset at how the community was being led, or more specifically, "not led," so I left.

I promised myself that if I were lucky enough to find a community that was looking for a new type of leader, one that had "heart," I would jump at the chance. After several other jobs, my patience paid off; I finally landed a position as senior level manager for a 55+ adult living community with an annual budget of $2 million a year. I was thrilled; I was finally in a position to implement my best employee engagement practices, which I had tweaked over several positions. Within just two years, enjoying 100 percent employee retention, my property was awarded "Property of the Year." Mission Possible!

I immediately began to engineer a completely reproducible set of guidelines that followed a distinct set of rules of engagement for senior living community leaders. I am passionate about this because it works and brings joy to all involved. A happy community is a successful community for both employees and residents. I am thrilled to present you with the results: *Hang on to Your Stars.* You are holding the key to employee retention in your hands. This book follows the same rules I have been teaching managers throughout my career and what I have implemented with my own staff. Through best practices, personal interviews, surveys, research, articles, significant white papers and books on the subject, I present you with a simple and effective step-by-step guide, and I am excited to share it with you. I will show you how to turn your new employees into stars and how to keep your current stars glowing. Pay special attention to the real-world stories that appear throughout the book in italics that illustrate important points. I wrote this guide to inspire you to make changes in the way you lead your community, and your results will be as powerful as mine.

The star symbol ✦ signifies a bright idea; feel free to use it. I can tell you from my professional experience, these ideas work!

To some readers, this book may seem like an oversimplification of terms, but that is its purpose. I am not interested in trying to impress you with the history of past engagement practices, business theories, or complicated psychological formulas on human behavior. This book will provide you with what it will take to engage, inspire, and retain your most valuable asset—your employees—without a big budget. Now, let me show you how to *hang on to your stars*!

Section I

Introduction—The Critical First 90 Days

"People work for money, but if you engage, support, and offer them praise, watch what happens!"

– Doreen A. Lang

Without exception, engaged and happy employees lie at the foundation of every successful senior living community. When employees are engaged, they align with business objectives, work harder, are more productive, and feel successful. However, employee retention has become a critical business challenge as the senior care industry continues to grow and currently faces serious, unprecedented workforce challenges. Simply stated, senior living has an engagement problem.

Findings reveal a caregiver shortage. Competition for outstanding employees is soaring along with a high turnover rate. The statistics are overwhelming as the number of people who require long-term care keeps rising, and the current available source of trained people to provide those services just can't keep up with the growing demands.

The United States will need between 2–3 million more workers by 2030 to provide long-term care to the aging population. At the same time, it must deal with the turnover crisis, which is estimated at 40–60 percent or higher, particularly in the first 90 days of employment. With the nationwide unemployment rate standing at only 4.6 percent at the time of this writing, the lowest it has been in a decade, opportunities abound in other less stressful fields. This compounds the difficulty in attracting and keeping good, qualified help. The annual turnover rate among health care workers is staggering. Some turnover is inevitable; people go back to school, get married, move away, get sick, or retire. However, retention has become an ongoing workforce challenge. In the health care industry more than one in five employees quit their jobs every year. Other industries experience an average of 12–15 percent turnover rate. This is a significant difference at a time when finding high-quality caretakers is as important as the number of workers needed.

In the first quarter of 2017, senior living, assisted living, and continuing care retirement communities had 21,000 open jobs.

And that number has increased by more than 3,000 since December 2016. By 2025, the health care industry will need to hire over 1 million new workers to care for the country's growth in its aging population.

This strong demand encourages employees to seek more attractive opportunities or higher pay. It is rarely possible for communities to increase pay and benefits for good workers due to cutbacks and controlled expenses; organizations need to look at new and creative ways to retain their employees and change their focus to see their employees as their greatest asset as never before. The business mantra used to be, "The customer is king," but not anymore. The mantra for business success, at least in the senior-care industry, has evolved into, "Employees are key."

In addition to senior living organizations needing to refocus their approach retaining their existing staff, they must also adapt to the needs and expectations of the incoming generational workers—the Millennials. This generation wants flexibility and life balance. They want to receive constant feedback and are looking for relationships with their supervisors to reflect more of a "work with," not a "work for," relationship. They have lofty expectations for their career goals and want more of a coach or mentor relationship for their development than the typical supervisor and subordinate relationship.

Staff retention can soar when the senior care community promotes a high level of engagement among its employees.

3

Highly successful leaders and managers who retain their resident care professionals know that paying attention to them and positively engaging them can greatly decrease turnover.

Unfortunately, we all think we will live forever. Most of us believe we will have enough money and will not need any additional help or services as we grow older. Some of us just don't want to think about growing older and needing a stranger's help. Therefore, we underestimate the likelihood that we will need long-term care, and we don't plan for the cost associated with it. While over a third of people over 50 years of age think they may need this care, the reality is that as many as 70 percent will.

During the late 1970s, the average American mother gave birth to 3.5 children. Since then family size has been on the decline. Now we see older women (over the age of 35) having children and having approximately one child on average.

Family size is shrinking. So, who will take care of us as we age? For our sakes, we can only hope it's a happy and engaged workforce because the demand for senior care will be significant.

Given these circumstances, senior living organizations need to focus on effective engagement practices and create an employee-centric environment, as well as a strong workforce committed to excellence. Organizations must look for ways to keep their employees engaged, give them reasons to stay and make it difficult for them to leave. This book will tell you exactly how you can do that.

Chapter 1

What Employee Engagement Is Not

From the moment you hire a new employee, a working relationship begins. But to foster employee engagement requires more effort than simply establishing a professional relationship. It involves the continual development of an emotional and professional relationship between the employee and the manager. It brings heart and mind into the holistic process. You, as the leader, play a critical role in creating workplace engagement that includes an emotional component you cannot overlook.

When employees are developed effectively, engagement practices build within their ranks. In a sense, they become captivated. A strong sense of commitment, dedication, and happiness develops. However, many organizations do not put enough emphasis on the first, critical 90 days with a well-organized introductory engagement plan to welcome new employees into the organization.

Below is an all-too-common (true) story of an unfortunate first day for a new employee. The names have been changed, but the details are accurate. Don't let this happen to any of your new employees…read on to the following chapters to learn how to create employee engagement success.

Mary Jacobs, a new hire, started her job with the usual first-day jitters. As she drove to her new position as a resident assistant for a highly established assisted living community, her anxiety got the best of her. She was a little excited but mostly nervous. As she pulled into the parking lot, she panicked. Where was she supposed to park? She had emailed her new boss Karen several days before and asked her where employees park, but never heard back from her. As she looked around, she got confused. Through which door was she supposed to enter? Why did it all look so different this morning? Was it the rain? She looked at her watch and had five minutes before she had to go in, so she tried to calm herself down as she drove around.

Finally, she saw an empty space next to the dumpsters in the back of the building. As she pulled in, she saw the trash truck coming toward her. She parked the car, shut it off, pulled out the keys, and was startled by the noise of a loud horn. She looked up and saw the angry face of the truck driver, who was waving his hands. She hurriedly stepped out of the car and called out to him, "What's wrong?"

"Move your car, lady. I gotta swing this thing around. You're in the way."

Mary got back in the car, started it, and drove back around the property. This time, she located a space closer to the building. She pulled in and then checked her watch. It was 8:00 a.m.—time to go in.

She grabbed her lunch bag and purse and ran into the building. When she finally stepped inside, she was drenched. She had forgotten her umbrella in the car and tried to look as though being soaked from the rain didn't matter. She was confused as she looked around. Things looked different from the day she had interviewed, but she kept walking until she saw someone who pointed her in the right direction. The receptionist welcomed her, and as they called her supervisor to come meet her, Mary asked to use the ladies' room. She knew she looked like a drowned rat and needed to dry off. As she hurried to the restroom, she looked at the clock on the wall. It was 8:10.

"Damn," she thought, *"I hope they don't think I was late."* Her heart sunk; she was cold, wet, and worried. After she dried off in the bathroom with paper towels and stuck her head under the hot-air blower, she scurried back to the desk. Waiting for her was a harried-looking woman she had never met.

"Hi," Mary said.

"Hello, I'm Cathy. Come with me."

Mary wasn't sure who this person was but she knew that keeping her waiting wasn't a good idea. As she walked down the hall behind her, she *felt ill. Nothing had gone right so far, and she thought, "Maybe this is a bad sign. Maybe this isn't going to work after all."*

Mary was taken to a small room with several tables, no windows, and frigid air conditioning. She was cold enough to envision icicles growing in her hair. She was shown where she could hang her coat and then Cathy sat down with her. "A few things," she said. "I am going to be your supervisor. Karen, who was supposed to be your boss, left the company last Friday. You need to be on time, and you need to come in the main entrance. Did you send Human Resources all the paperwork they asked for?" Mary said she had done that over a week ago. "Good," Cathy said and then told Mary that she had a long video to watch. "After you watch the first video, you need to hit the pause button and then take the quiz. You will have about five or six videos. When you are all done, bring them back to me with this clipboard. My office is across the hall."

Mary thanked her as Cathy handed her the remote and walked away. As Mary sat there alone with the remote control in her hand she thought, "What am I doing here? Is this their idea of training? This is awful."

By the time Mary watched all the videos and took the quizzes, it was 11:30 a.m. She stood up, walked over to the TV, and turned it off. She needed to visit the bathroom and was very thirsty, but she wanted Cathy to know she was done. She figured she would ask her where the restroom was when she saw her. As Mary approached Cathy's office, she could hear Cathy was on the phone.

Mary entered the office and sat down. She put the clipboard on Cathy's desk, whispered that she was going to the bathroom, and left. She looked up and down the hallway, but didn't venture too far as she was afraid she would get lost. After heading down several hallways, there were no restrooms to be found. When Mary returned to the office, Cathy was still on the phone, so she sat back down.

It was 11:55 by the time Mary's supervisor hung up the phone. She expected Cathy to apologize for making her wait so long while she was on the call, but she just said something under her breath, thumbed through some papers, and without looking up said, "So, how was it?"

"Interesting," Mary said.

Cathy stood up, still making no eye contact, and said, "Ok, let's stop at Human Resources and see Kim, and then I will take you to the lunchroom."

Mary was relieved. She was hungry and thirsty and wanted to get away from her new boss, even for a few minutes. As they walked to Human Resources, Mary said hello to residents and employees and felt good when she got a smile in return. The Human Resources office was closed, so Cathy murmured, "They must be at lunch or out, or whatever. Let me show you the lunchroom."

As they walked through the hallway, a male employee approached Cathy and asked a question about a training that was supposed to take place that week. She responded sharply with, "You will have to check your email. It was sent out yesterday." The employee looked embarrassed, and Mary felt bad for him. "Why did Cathy have to be so rude?" she thought. She caught the man's eye and smiled at him understandingly. He just glanced at her, and walked away. Cathy turned to Mary, looking directly at her for the first time, and said, "He's new, and he just seems to act as dumb as he did on his first day."

Mary was upset and confused and thought, "Is this what she thinks about me too?" She had a bad feeling that would not go away about this new company.

She followed Cathy through a large set of double doors and, with one hand, Cathy shoved them open. The room was brightly lit, filled with people and voices from employees talking on their phones or with each other. Cathy stopped, turned to Mary, and said, "You will have to find your way around; I need to make some calls." She pointed across the room and said, "There is fresh food in that fridge and packaged food in the cabinets. There is a microwave if you want to heat up anything. If you want something cooked, do it quickly. We have more training this afternoon."

Worried, Mary asked, "More videos?" She hoped there would be more valuable orientation offered that day.

"Yes, the afternoon videos are about kitchen cleanliness and food safety." Cathy said, "See you at 12:30."

Before Mary walked away, She asked Cathy, "When do you think I might get on the floor or meet some residents? I am excited to get to work."

Cathy looked at her for a long minute and said, "You are an aggressive one, aren't you? Don't worry about that right now. We have a lot of training to do before then."

Feeling like she may have been too pushy, Mary thanked her and stepped farther into the room, and when she looked back, Cathy was gone.

She scanned the room for an empty seat, saw a few, but felt awkward and out of place. Why didn't Cathy at least introduce her to someone she could sit with? She felt like such an outsider.

Mary walked over to the refrigerator and noticed a restroom near it. She needed the bathroom badly and wanted to send a text to her boyfriend in private. She walked over to the door and turned the knob, but it was locked. Feeling frustrated and uncomfortable, she sat down and waited. A few minutes later, a woman came out and Mary ran in. She texted her boyfriend, "THIS PLACE IS AWFUL. MY BOSS IS A NASTY ROBOT. AND NOW I AM SUPPOSED TO EAT ALONE WITH A GROUP OF STRANGERS. I FEEL LIKE I AM INVISIBLE," and hit "Send."

When Mary left the bathroom, she walked to the fridge, but just before she opened the door to remove a bottle of water, she stopped. She thought about the remains of her morning tea that were sitting in her car's cup holder. She sat in an empty seat near the door and tried to catch the eye of people around her with a friendly smile, but no one smiled back. It was as if they didn't see her—as if she really were invisible!

Mary had never felt so bad at a new job in her life. She knew she had made a big mistake, and this was not the place for her. She returned to the training room, retrieved her coat, and walked down the hall toward the exit sign. Without looking back, she slipped out the door.

When she reached her car, she got in and took a glorious sip of her leftover tea. Even though it was cold, it was comforting. As she started the engine, she felt a sweeping sense of relief. She was glad to escape the cold building, her disinterested boss, and her own feelings of insignificance.

"I hope to God the residents are treated better than I was," she thought. She picked up her phone and sent another text to her boyfriend—"HORRIBLE PLACE, HORRIBLE WOMAN, I'M DONE."

Many organizations are inept at acclimating and integrating new employees. For example, some organizations attempt the following onboarding plan: Day 1—the new hires begin work, and management or a designated representative introduces them to a few key staff members and shows them where to hang their coats. Then they are plopped in front of a video, which introduces them to safety regulations that may or may not pertain to them. Finally, the new hires return to their respective departments where they must figure out things on their own.

During the year, your organization might throw a few holiday parties and send out birthday cards. It is typical, but not necessarily the case, that it may also host an annual all-staff meeting. But this **does not** constitute engagement. If Mary's example or what I've described is your "onboarding process," it could spell disaster for both your organization and your new hires.

New employees who are left to their own devices early on will often change the way they look and feel about their positions. If they feel left behind and abandoned to figure things out for themselves, they will quickly become unsure of what is expected of them and begin to disengage. The chance they will last beyond their first day is slim and they will likely leave within the first 90 days.

Mary's experience is more common than you think. In researching hundreds of publications about employees' first-day experiences in their new positions, the statistics were startling. Ninety-four percent of new employees had less-than-desirable first-day experiences, and many had horror stories to share. The typical story revealed the following common occurrences. The new employees were introduced to a few staff members, their schedules were discussed, and they were shown where their personal items were to be kept. Some organizations went so far as to show them the location of the bathroom, and after the property tour, they were left alone. It is no wonder that 40 percent of new employees leave their positions within the first 90 days—especially those who are in the roles of caretakers. These new hires need the most attention and introduction during onboarding to be able to feel confident they can provide the quality care that is expected of them.

If your organization extends only the basic onboarding practices, I am thrilled you are reading this book. It will take you through steps to change your course now and put in place an engagement plan that works!

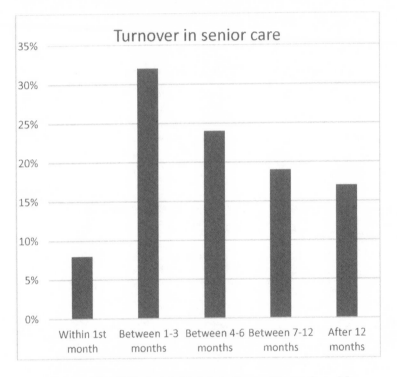

Source: OnShift & McKnight's Long-Term Care News Survey—When Turnover Occurs

Chapter 2

Why Employees Leave

What happens in the first 90 days of employment that causes so many employees to leave?

The main reasons include:

1. **Uncertain expectations:** When expectations from the department manager or organization are not clear from the beginning, new employees are put in a position to think on their own and assume what's expected. This causes frustration and confusion for all involved.

2. **Personal conflict:** If a new hire doesn't get along with his or her manager or coworkers, it can prove disastrous. Positive relationships and compatibility are

key for employee engagement. If there is a conflict that exists, and he or she feels disconnected from the team, the new hire might believe there is no future in that community.

3. **Lack of training:** When new hires don't get the training they need, they are likely to feel they don't have what it takes to be successful, and they will get out before they find themselves underwater. Training is often the major objective in taking a position in their area of interest. If they don't get training or realize the organization puts little emphasis on learning, they may feel the position is a dead end.

4. **Feeling unwanted:** Employees who don't receive time or attention from their manager or aren't able to connect with other colleagues, thus feeling isolated and unhappy, are more likely to leave.

It's noteworthy that you can completely avoid the situations that cause new employees to leave. Communication and connections are the primary drivers of engagement success. When the recruitment process is tied together tightly with the community's mission, values, and expectations, new employees have a solid chance to feel engaged. They will better understand their role and how it fits into the culture of the community.

Chapter 3

Real Costs and Impacts of Employee Turnover

Turnover costs

Turnover across all U.S. jobs costs approximately $5 trillion annually. This cost is avoidable. Leaders and managers know it's easier and less costly to keep motivation going than to let it die. But whether you are aware of that fact or not, if you are dealing with constant turnover, this book is for you. It will show you how to build an engagement plan that encourages employees at all levels to work together and embrace whatever it takes to get the job done.

Financial impact

Studies predict the cost to replace a salaried employee is around six to nine months of the employee's salary. For example, for a manager who makes $60,000 a year, the business spends $30,000–$45,000 in recruitment and training costs alone for a new employee. Some studies suggest the cost is even higher, up to double the employee's annual salary. That's revenue down the drain—money that could go toward raises, supplies, and/or improving conditions for the residents.

The list of financial costs to replace an employee is long. There is often severance pay, higher unemployment taxes, cost of outsourcing temporary help, insourcing temporary help by paying overtime, advertising, recruitment fees, background checks, drug tests, hiring bonuses, travel, and relocations costs. Supplemental training costs include additional training and development programs, special certifications, on-the-job training, new uniforms, and more. Studies have found the average replacement costs are as follows:

- A $10 per hour employee—more than $3,000
- A nurse—$50,000
- An experienced critical care nurse—$120,000

No business can afford a revolving door of talent, least of all, the health care and senior care industries. Turnover may vary by wage and role of employee, but the evidence clearly demonstrates the costs are just too high to be sustainable.

Motivational costs

The intangible costs of training, retraining, lost productivity, resident care errors, and cultural impacts are difficult to track but are just as critical to the team and the community. When an employee leaves an organization, other employees stop and ask, "Why?" They usually respond by immediately disengaging while they grapple with the loss. During this disengagement, the organization suffers from lost productivity because their attention and focus are diverted. Employees feel unmotivated when they lose a team member. They often experience the loss as sad, unsettling, and disruptive to their own work. The left-behind employees start asking, "Is it time for me to move on, too? I wonder if my coworker's new community is better? Should I brush up my resume and look around?"

The change is disruptive and disconcerting, even if employees know the circumstances surrounding their co-worker's departure. The left-behind employees begin to feel anxious about how the absence will affect them. They may also fear management will place more of a burden on them to pick up additional duties and responsibilities until a new person is on board and trained. You want employees to be happily engaged so they won't look around. Then, you will be able to keep them.

Chapter 4

The Dangers of Disengagement

With Millennials quickly dominating the workplace, let's see how engaged they are.

Source: Gallup News. Few Millennials are Engaged at Work.

71%	Millennials actively checked out
29%	Millennials engaged

As you can see, disengagement is high—dangerously high if you want to retain your staff. I wouldn't be surprised if these disengaged people have one eye on job postings and one foot out the door.

It's interesting that disengagement and disenchantment are palpable in the workplace; it is not a "hidden syndrome." An outsider can walk into a department and instantly sense engaged, happy, and communicative employees—and the feeling is contagious.

In addition to the negative, unproductive atmosphere disengagement creates, problems and mistakes often occur as a direct result of unfocused and disengaged employees. How many mistakes do these employees generate? One is too many. Mistakes in senior living can be life-threatening, so the stakes are higher than in other industries.

In this book, you will learn the strategies to successfully engage employees. I want to impress upon you right now just how realistic it is for you to become a successful leader with an engaged, committed, and happy staff and enjoy off-the-chart retention rates. However, you need to follow the steps in this guide and change the management paradigm. The engagement process is more natural and holistic than you can imagine, and putting "heart" back into business equates to a successful business. The strategies are simple, but they are not always easy to implement when working from the old paradigm. Einstein was right when he said, "The mind is like a parachute; it only works when it's open." It is easier for those leaders who can open their minds and make a commitment to the plan.

So, once you make the commitment to incorporate engagement into your organization as a fundamental component of your overall plan and put in place the resources necessary to manage this process, you will succeed. Or, you can go about *business as usual* and hope for the best with a style of management I call "ostrich management." This style allows you to stick your head in the sand and hope for the best without taking any action. You have experienced the pain of losing employees too often, so here is your chance to take control of the process and focus on an engagement plan for your employees to help them become the stars you can hang on to.

A high-profit organization with low engagement is like a boat without an engine. It's only a matter of time before disaster strikes.

Chapter 5

Employee Engagement is the Key to Success

Leaders have a critical 90-day window of time to onboard and drive an engagement program to create a happy and productive new employee who will benefit the organization. So, let's look at what engagement is all about.

There are many definitions of employee engagement, including the highlights below:

- Having clear expectations.

- Understanding their position is fundamental to the organization's purpose and objectives.

- Feeling supported, encouraged to build on their skills, and appreciated for the work they do.

- Having access to training and professional development.

- Having a deeper commitment to the team, which results in few sick days, conflicts, and complaints.
- Feeling proud to be a part of their team and to work for a supportive manager.

To hire and retain some of the best health care professionals means you must create a different kind of plan to attract Millennials. You'll need to identify and utilize varied recruiting avenues like never before. To reach out and know where they learn and play is the key to learning the language of this emerging demographic. With technology as their first language, they are all connected and just a click away. Social media is a highly effective and often the easiest way to reach out and connect with them.

Engagement is about a lot of things, but the bottom line is that employees who believe that an organization genuinely cares about them and wants them to develop professionally are more productive, content, and fulfilled. This creates a *domino* effect: Engagement leads to a happy and productive workforce; subsequently, employee retention equals quality resident care.

The table below shows you how engagement pays off:

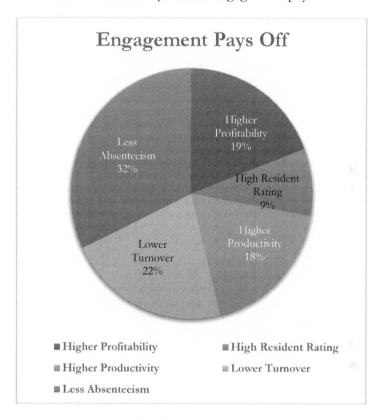

Engagement Pays Off

- Higher Profitability 19%
- High Resident Rating 9%
- Higher Productivity 18%
- Lower Turnover 22%
- Less Absenteeism 32%

■ Higher Profitability   ■ High Resident Rating

■ Higher Productivity   ■ Lower Turnover

■ Less Absenteeism

Source: Gallup Workplace. Drive Employee Engagement.

In any relationship, we all ask the same questions:

1. What am I getting?
2. What am I giving?
3. Do I belong here?
4. Am I in it for the long haul?
5. How can I continue to develop?
6. Am I happy?

It's no different for employees in the workplace. They want to be part of a community where they are happy and successfully engaged in the work they love alongside people they respect and enjoy.

Chapter 6

Millennials—The Next Generation of Leaders

Two people are in a focus group in an Apple store. One is a Boomer, and one is a Millennial. The sales clerk walks over to them, hands each of them the newest Apple device and says, "Play with this awhile, and I'll be back." The sales clerk returns 15 minutes later and asks, "Well, what do you think?"

The Boomer says, "What does this do?"

The Millennial says, "What else can it do?"

As a leader, you face the critical task of attracting and developing the next generation of leaders. You will find these stars when you go on a galaxy quest, but you will have to be creative and passionate about your mission and vision as you communicate your message to this emerging demographic.

Before we go any further, let me give you the general parameters on which most researchers will agree. The generations fall into these basic categories:

- Baby Boomers I, born 1946–1955, were in or protested the Vietnam War.
- Boomers II, born 1956–1964

The total Boomer I and II generations make up about 71 million people.

- Generation X, born 1965–1980, aka. "latchkey kids," 49 million
- Generation Y, born 1981–1997, aka. "echo" or "Millennials," 70 million
- Generation Z, born 1997–2012, 23 million

Thousands of Boomers are reaching retirement age every day, and that trend will continue through the next decade. Roughly 10,000 people are turning 65 every day between now and 2030. Many more in this demographic will need to move to senior living in the approaching years, and facilities will need to expand and strengthen their staffs to meet the growing demands of this bourgeoning industry.

Millennials, or the emerging leader born in the 1980s and '90s, are the children of Baby Boomers and older Gen Xers. By the end of this decade, this emerging leader will make up more than half of the workforce. By 2030, they will represent approximately 75 percent of the workforce. Stop and think about that. It means hiring and retaining the best of the best, which means learning about and responding to what makes Millennials tick.

Make no mistake—Millennials' expectations and demands are different from those of the Baby Boomer generations. One of the Millennial generation's top priorities is to find employment that allows balance between their private and professional lives. The organization needs to respond to their personal needs and professional development, or they will ultimately reject the status quo and move on. Unlike Boomers, they don't value the working propositions of acceptance, persistence, and patience.

Important differences appear between the Boomers and the later generations—the Gen Xers and Millennials. The Millennials are the first generation to grow up with computers in their homes. Some Gen Xers and many Boomers rely predominantly on their cable TV universe, while Millennials prefer streaming content over the internet. Many of them access shows on TV only as a means of connecting socially when they gather or when watching something on a device (smartphone, tablet, or laptop) proves logistically challenging. They will watch a sports event on television, since a large TV screen offers a more real-time experience. When they're alone, they return to their devices for live shows, music, and movies. Unlike Boomers, they prefer to get their news on the internet, subscribing to online publications and following Twitter, Facebook, and Instagram to get up-to-date data and drama.

The Millennials' method of viewing information and entertainment differs significantly from the way Boomers experience them. Boomers grew up with a TV set that had three major stations, rabbit ear antennas and very blurry reception. In the Boston area, Channel 2 (public broadcasting), which wasn't really considered a station, was more of a news station. Then there were Channels 4, 5, and 7. The TV reception was terrible, at best, with most programs covered in a fuzzy backdrop of snow. And most people had only black-and-white TVs. Color TVs eventually came on the scene, but adoption was slow. Once consumers started buying them, additional channels appeared. Boomers still rent videos; they don't stream as much as younger generations. They still go to movies and even to libraries to pick up a DVD. Computers were for businesses, not for homes, and the telephone was wall-mounted. The only way to make the phone portable was to install a very long cord so you could walk around and move from room to room.

A few days ago, I was at a restaurant having dinner, and a small child ran by me with a long TV remote in his hand. He must have picked it up off the hostess's station. The little boy went running by, pressing it up against his ear. He thought it was a cell phone. It's an amazing, changing world.

As a community manager, I still find homes with people born in the late '20s and '30s who have a landline phone with a long cord. Many of these same people carry a cell phone, only because they were forced to do so by their kids so they could keep tabs on their parents' whereabouts. But these older residents often forget to carry or charge their phones—old habits die hard. The Boomers still have trouble adopting new technology. When a Boomer is tech savvy, the usual comment is, "Wow, that's great. Where did you learn it?" And the usual answer is, "My kids."

I was getting my car repaired the other day and found myself sitting in the waiting room of the auto shop. There was a little girl running around who couldn't have been more than three years old. I have a fondness for small children, so I set my book down and watched her. Her mother was sitting in the chair across from me, talking to her about this and that. Then her mother said, "Chloe, can you help me find the clicker? I want to change this news station and find something you can watch."

The little girl walked over to the old, dusty TV, stopped and stood in front of it. Then she raised her right hand and gently swiped at the picture on the screen. I was stunned. I looked at her mother, but she was still watching her daughter. She politely said, "Chloe, it doesn't work that way," and Chloe looked back at her mother and said, "It's old, Mama."

This was a first for me. In that instant, I felt ancient and in awe of this little girl. Her expectations were to be able to manipulate the screen and change the picture by swiping it. Next thing you know, she will be able to Facetime the TV. Talk about a new generation in a new world!

For their communal needs, Millennials use social networking sites, such as Twitter, Facebook, Snapchat, and dozens of others to make new acquaintances and remain connected with friends and family. Families everywhere use Skype and FaceTime to communicate with their children in colleges all over the world. How fantastic to be able to see your loved one's face instantly. This is their normal. You can be sure that the children set up Skype on their parents' devices and taught them how to use it. It is no wonder this generation, known for an increased use and understanding of electronic communications, media, and technologies, is also known as "Digital Natives." Technology is their second language.

The Millennials look at their jobs as a series of steps to get where they want to be. Boomers change jobs, on average, every five years. For Millennials, it is every two. So, how do organizations recruit, hire, and retain the next generation of leaders? We can do it by understanding what motivates and engages them and by modifying the workplace to meet their motivators.

Chapter 7

What's Motivating Millennials?

Millennials want to work in an environment that is an extension of their social connections. They want collaborative environments with teamwork to be the norm. They want to work in what they call a "fun" workplace that provides a unique experience. For instance, putting a juice bar in the lunchroom may sound far-fetched or frivolous, but organizations must be creative and innovative to capture their interest and add that special something to create the social engagement component they desire and expect.

They expect professional development and training, coupled with the opportunity to move ahead swiftly. They are ambitious and want to move up—or they'll move out. They will not stick around if they don't see things moving as quickly or as focused *on them* as they would like.

Their managers need to be involved in their learning and to respond if they see a lack of motivation. One way to keep them engaged is to offer more challenging work. Millennials are coming into positions highly educated and culturally diverse. Organizations need to offer intergenerational education to create strong bonds among the Millennials and their Boomer and Gen X residents and coworkers. Allow the generations to learn with and from one another and to work side-by-side.

Conduct inverse trainings. Ask Millennials to teach the Boomers. Set up trainings with the Millennials as teachers and allow them to teach computer technology and social networking to the Boomers to help close the technology gap between the generations. When these generations work together and learn about each other, it creates a natural camaraderie between them, something necessary to work effectively and comfortably as a team.

Reaching Millennials through local educational programs is smart business, as is recruiting early. For example, holding subsidized training programs through high school and community colleges cultivates fertile recruiting grounds. Organizations should conduct focus groups with Millennials to learn exactly what motivates them to work in senior care and how they feel they can make a difference.

✦ Leverage their knowledge and apply it. Conduct "Millennial Madness Meetings" with Millennial employees to continue to learn about them and learn from them. For these meetings, put a bowl of M&M's (Management & Millennials) on the table. The humor and the sweets can't hurt! Tell them you want to hear all their ideas and ask them to shoot for the stars. Instruct them to put their phones on airplane mode!

✦ Establish a corporate university. Add your current trainings and combine any other assessment tools, skills training, product introductions, etc., and brand them to your organization. Give the university a name and make it part of your organization's corporate culture. When you require all employees to go through the university, leaders can be sure training is consistent across the board. Once an employee has completed the core training, issue a diploma. As you add advanced courses, you can use a leaderboard to recognize their progress through higher levels of trainings.

Technology is their language, so give your millennial employees the technology they need to be part of an organization that values current technological systems and makes them feel at home. If it takes updating your archaic internal processing systems to engage this generation, you are on the right track. Ultimately, it will create more efficiencies in the process; just go ask them.

Significant and meaningful work is important to Millennials. They want purpose. Their generation is socially and environmentally responsible. They want to discuss issues and expect to be a part of the solutions. Social media has promised them that anything is possible, and they want to be part of great things that affect people and the world. They want to work in teams and collaborate on critical issues. They want to be viewed as important members who add value to the organization's bottom line, regardless of their position.

Millennials place great importance on being able to work without being micromanaged. The technical resources available to this generation have enabled them to become extremely independent. Through digital connectivity, they can find solutions and opportunities on their own as well as make new connections. They look for employers who listen and value their input, regardless of their positions within the organization. They want to receive regular feedback, positive reinforcement, and be recognized and rewarded based on their contributions. Above all, they look for opportunities to lead, create, and innovate. Millennials seek more feedback, responsibilities, and involvement in decision-making. Managers need to create an environment where they feel supported, valued, and reassured that their positive results will accrue to their benefit.

Millennials want to be a part of a socially communicative organization. They have learned to use social media as a means for seeking opportunities and sharing ideas. This stimulates them, and they expect to be a part of those circles. They not only want to make the world a better place, they believe they can.

Provide community-wide volunteer days to create an engaged team-based company culture. Millennials look beyond pay and benefits and focus on a company's work culture. Corporate volunteerism should be part of the over-all strategy to keep employees happy while building an engaged workforce.

They look for low-cost health-benefit packages that include high-quality insurance plans. They expect healthy incentive programs with the ability to manage their benefits on their own through digital tools. Comprehensive benefit programs that include additional perks, such as discounts to local gyms, health programs that focus on preventive care, etc., are their expectation and the norm for this generation.

Millennials expect a constant dialogue about the organization's plans, changes, and goals. When you offer opportunities for mentorship and coaching, you create an environment that fosters connections and opportunities. Millennials are looking for companies that care about the future of the world and care about their professional growth. They want to work *with*, not *for*, their supervisors.

Chapter 8

Millennial Interviews: What Makes Them Tick?

I conducted interviews with Millennials born from 1981–1992 to learn what engages them. I wanted to know if there was still more to learn that the data did not show. And the results were very interesting. I surveyed 50 Millennials from all backgrounds and levels of education and asked them the same questions. Below are results from the *few that represented the majority.*

The responses below are unedited. Participants include the following professions: environmental consultant, nurse practitioner, teacher, fifth-year Ph.D. student in applied physics, teacher's aide, lawyer, hotel front office manager, Trader Joe's crew member, special educational paraprofessional, salesperson, product manager, and assistant project manager. All participants

have been working in their roles for approximately two months
to less than three years.

1. What about your job makes you get out of bed in the morning?

"I am currently seeking a new job and am not satisfied with
my company's culture, so the primary driver for me at my
current job is my paycheck. However, when I have been more
excited about my job, one of the main motivators for me has
been getting to work with intelligent people on interesting
projects."

"I have to be there early to feel prepared and ready for my
day. If I do not get there early enough, I start my day off on the
wrong foot and never feel quite "caught up.""

"A combination of not wanting to be late and getting fired
and the hope that it leads to a better ultimate career."

"I like the people I work with and the company itself, since
it's fast paced and I'm always learning something new."

"Being able to interact with people while I work makes my
job enjoyable. I look forward to seeing familiar faces in the
workplace."

2. What makes you hit the snooze button?

"I dread going into work when I know that there is an issue
looming due to poor organization within my company, such as
a project that is over budget or unreasonable deadlines."

"Not wanting to get up in the cold room in winter, and wanting a little more rest before I start a busy day."

"I am still not 100% sure of what I want, and it is still hard for me to be motivated to get up."

"I'm typically not a morning person, so I always hit the snooze button once so I can be fully awake."

"Sleeping is the easy option in my opinion. Laziness and the thought that I can't binge watch Netflix at work makes me hit the snooze button."

3. If you were to win the Megabucks and leave your position, what would you miss the most about your job?

"I would miss the opportunity to challenge myself and solve problems while working on projects. It can be very gratifying to solve a puzzle that you've been piecing together for several days or weeks!"

"I would miss having a schedule, learning new things daily, seeing familiar faces, and laughing with co-workers. The top thing would be relationships with others, but I'm sure I'd find that elsewhere."

"I would definitely stay in touch with my boss and my other team members. I work with good people."

"I like having a consistent schedule and using my education to my advantage."

"I'd miss that rush of understanding, and my identity of being "a physicist." I actually took a gap year between college and graduate school and did work that had absolutely nothing to do with science or with physics but I found myself missing it so much that I actually did physics problems in my spare time, and hung around the University of Chicago's physics department, just to try to re-solidify that aspect of my identity."

4. What would make you consider leaving this job?

"I am currently considering leaving my job because I think the culture of my company does not promote a good work-life balance and also can set up people for failure through mismanaged budgets, deadlines, etc."

"Not knowing who my assistant will be, so that day to day, I'm wondering who my support staff is, forcing me to figure it out myself."

"If they just threw me into meetings and into the spotlight without getting me totally comfortable with everything. It is a lot of pressure and very confusing still."

"If my time was micromanaged."

"If my advisor said I wasn't ready to graduate next year, or had to stay for three more years or something, I would seriously consider just giving up and not getting my degree. Additionally, if she became outwardly dismissive of my work or prevented me from publishing it, that would become a toxic environment that might force me to leave."

5. If you could, what would be the one thing you would change about your department, team, or organization?

"I would like to shift the focus from profitability to making a good product. Oftentimes people end up caring so much about the budget that they rush through a project and tend to miss important findings, produce a report that does not look good or read well."

"I would improve the management–make it more interactive and responsive."

"The ability to work together a little bit better and communicate. Certain things happen sometimes when only a few people know what is going on, and if it were better communicated, mistakes or misunderstandings could be avoided."

"I wish they had more time to train and get people familiar with the roles. Also for them to take the time to explain things and use code words/nicknames for things."

"It is difficult to get promoted within, so I would like to see more promotions for people that are working hard."

6. What could your manager do a little more of or less of?

"My manager could micromanage less. Sometimes when he thinks a task isn't being done fast enough he will take back an assignment and do it himself. The reason many of his employees may not prioritize a task is due to a miscommunication or simply because they are so busy they don't have enough time in the day. He could also benefit from being more proactive when it comes to learning new technology instead of pinning simple tasks, like converting a word document to a pdf, on younger hires so that they have more free time to learn job-related skills."

"My manager could check in with me more. As of now, she doesn't reach out unless she has to. It would be nice to have meetings, even just 1–2x per year, one-on-one for work-related issues."

"Some more time explaining the reasoning and workings of things instead of just handing me piece rate tasks."

"I wish that my advisor would meet more often with the people in her lab, myself included, and make more time for us. I also sometimes feel that she is impatient with work that does not produce flashy results and dismissive of some of our efforts, so I wish she afforded us a little more respect."

"My manager should interact with his employees more, provide us with more feedback, and be there when we need his assistance."

7. If you had to return to a previous position, which one would it be and why?

"I would return to working for a bank because I think that banks have better work-life balance, at least from what I experienced. People tend to be able to work a straight 8-hour shift and not feel obligated to answer emails outside of work hours. I think this gives everyone's brain a little more time off, which is important when you are trying to keep people excited about coming into work each day."

"I would go back to Starbucks. I liked the fast pace and personal interactions and how mostly young people worked there."

"I would most likely go back to my previous role, since I was dealing with several different teams across our company internationally and in Europe. It was great experience working with diverse groups."

"I would go back to my days as a busser at the Barker Tavern. One of my favorite things about the job was the dinner we were given every night. Free food at a high-quality restaurant was priceless to me."

"I would go back to be a summer camp counselor because it was great being paid to play all day, and there was a wonderful sense of teamwork and friendship amongst my coworkers."

8. What do you need to learn to work at your best?

"A supportive supervisor who is willing to listen to your concerns and to bounce ideas off. Learning from someone who has been in this field longer than me is reassuring."

"I like to learn how things work and have some on-the-job training to get me up to speed and understanding things I do best like that."

"To work at my best, I need to learn how to work alongside all different types of people. I cannot become discouraged and less efficient due to the personalities of my co-workers."

"I need a comfortable environment and a support system that lets me think on my own, while also providing me with guidance and care, if need. I am at my best when I have these two things in my life."

"I need an environment where I can learn from the people above me and where there is room for growth and new knowledge."

9. What makes for a great day?

"A well-paced schedule so I'm never behind, a few good interactions with patients or coworkers, and when patients are not rude to me."

"A great day is when I feel fully satisfied knowing that I did a good day's work and that my work was appreciated by the customer."

"When everyone else is in a good mood and there is something exciting going on that breaks us out of our routine day."

"A day filled with adventure and learning with a great group of people. Sharing learning experiences and being able to recall those moments or memories is what makes a day great for me."

"A good night's sleep, my best friend is at the office; I'm busy with work but not overwhelmed, and I interact with my boss about the work."

10. What could your manager do to make your job more satisfying?

"I would benefit from more autonomy and less micromanaging"

"Ask me at regular intervals how they can better support my success there, mostly to incentivize me to stay."

"My manager could give me hope for future possibilities and explain what my work could lead to within the company and my future."

"My manager could be more encouraging and maybe compliment us more to make the job more satisfying."

"Encourage staff get-togethers."

"Provide a few more opportunities where the whole department is together. I learn a ton from them when we are in department meetings and work groups. A few more opportunities to learn from each other would be great."

11. What could your manager do to support your career goals?

"He could make it easier for me to connect with those higher up in the company who could mentor me."

"He could motivate me more by describing the career path I can take and the potential rewards down the road."

"To support my career goals, my manager could provide additional access to training programs for certification in the field."

"My manager could provide more feedback on my progress and point out my weaknesses so I can improve upon them."

"Give me more substantive work and take the time to walk me through assignments I've never done before so I can learn how to do them."

12. Do you get recognized for the work you do? How do you like to be recognized?

"I believe that I get a fair amount of recognition. I like to be recognized simply by my manager saying to me, "Hey, great job today." Something as simple as that goes a long way."

"I believe I get enough recognition from my manager. I always want to be assured that my work is satisfactory and if there are any improvements that can be made to better myself."

"I don't think I get enough recognition. I'd like it if my advisor acknowledged the work that I do in the lab, and let me know what she thought of the quality of my research and ideas. More generally, all I want is to be thanked by my peers for when I help them out or talk with them about an idea or lend them code. A thank you is a surprisingly difficult thing to come by in some environments."

"My supervisor sends an email at least once every two weeks thanking us for the job we do, and reaches out when she knows we've had a stressful few days."

"Yes, I get enough recognition. I like to be pulled aside and privately recognized or encouraged."

13. What would you like to learn this year?

"I would like to learn more about the business aspects, such as accounting and other elements of project management, that I haven't had a chance to delve into yet."

"I always want to gain more medical knowledge and more knowledge about the health care system. I'd also like to learn how not to let patients who are very rude, difficult, demeaning, or sexist, otherwise unpleasant, affect my mood."

"I want to learn to be more productive and to become a more effective manager."

"How to be a better manager."

"I want to learn more about the framework for a complex litigation and I want to learn more about briefs."

So, what have we learned? From the responses above, you can see that Millennials value teamwork, training and expect professional development and advancement. They want respect and to advance—now. They also value praise, raises, and perks. Most are motivated financially, but there is more to this generation than meets the eye. In addition to subscribing to Millennials' needs and interests, pay close attention to *their* questions during interviews. These could well be very telling about what *they* expect in the workplace.

Engaging this dynamic demographic is a dance between art and science. Leaders and managers need to adjust their thinking about how to engage Millennials to build relationships for the best retention possible. Since they look for immediate feedback, expect to coach and train them to fulfill their desire to be challenged. Managers need to identify creative and aggressive engagement tactics to connect and stay in touch with this demographic in order to retain this confident, new employee.

With poor numbers reflecting the incoming generation of Millennials into senior living facilities, recruiting practices haven't met the challenge of communicating the importance of career opportunities in the industry. We need to do much more to attract this emerging generation. In the effort to plan and attract this critical workforce, senior living organizations are working hard to establish and support relationships with local cities and towns, working with schools and higher-education institutions to educate and attract younger generations of workers. Engaging students on projects that address various industry challenges, such as strategies to prevent falls, skills training, and medical product development, will help students understand the challenges the industry is facing. This will lay the groundwork to encourage more Millennials to learn about workforce opportunities.

Less than 25 percent of Millennials said they would consider a career in senior living. They cite inadequate pay as a major reason. This is disconcerting because salaries are not necessarily going to improve, and the need for care is increasing. So how will you address this?

Leaders need to throw out their current rule book of recruiting practices and pick up a recruiting book written by a Millennial. They need to find new, appealing, and engaging ways to attract this emerging demographic by adopting Millennials' perspectives to the fullest extent possible. Get up to speed with all the technology outlets and be sure to post open positions on Facebook, Twitter, LinkedIn, and other relevant social media hot spots. You'd better start to speak their language, or you'll be talking to yourself!

Section II

Traits Necessary for Engagement

You have the key to employee engagement in your hands. There is only one thing that precedes the changes necessary to create an engaging, fantastic workplace environment: It is the decision to lead as the CEO, or the *Chief Engagement Officer*. But how do you accomplish this? Below I outline the traits necessary to create a community that is teeming with passion, support, and accountable employees who feel they are important and make a difference—every day!

You set the tone; you set the pace; and you set the bar for the place. Everything you say, don't say, do, and don't do— employees are watching. It is about how you dress, what you laugh at, what you talk about, and yes, what you eat! Your employees are watching you closely, and your words and movements communicate what you stand for and what you value. Employees will mimic their supervisors if they want to either rise in their positions or just want to be more like them. It is not uncommon for employees to start dressing and speaking like their boss, and even drinking the same kind of coffee their boss drinks. Choose your words carefully and wisely. Be cognizant that you are communicating with every decision you make and every decision you don't make. Be unwavering in your communication about the organization's mission, values, and goals.

Employees need to hear these messages over and over. They need and want to believe in them. They need to feel proud of whom and what they work for. Be

Serve your team and convince them that your community is unique— because of them.

fair, be firm, but never mean. Have fun, enjoy them, tolerate mistakes, take risks, and share sacrifices. Serve your team and convince them that your community is unique—because of them.

Learning leaders find effective ways to create an engaged organization filled with smart and passionate employees who love to learn and feel part of something extraordinary and important. This exciting process takes great effort on your behalf but pays great dividends. Are you ready to put on a new set of glasses and see your role as one of a devoted champion for your stars? The following chapters in this section list the traits and describe the characteristics you need as the learning leader to communicate authenticity and devotion to your employees, which creates an engaging workplace.

Chapter 9

Lead by Example

A powerful way to demonstrate your genuine interest and commitment to improve your community's engagement is through learning. Learning starts with you and your managers' commitment to your own discovery and growth. It requires curiosity and drive to make it happen. Transform your energy for learning into action; pull the employees forward with you to explore new territories with increased results. Be a walking, talking example of what it takes to learn and stay current.

Be an aggressive learner. It is the single most powerful message you can send. Become the epitome of the teacher/learner model. Learn by teaching and teach by learning. Stay restless, always turning the page, looking for ways to improve your community. Pick up tips and use lessons from wherever you find them.

Without committing to learning, an organization will never approach its potential for success. The question you should continue to ask is, "What more can we do?" It is never, "Have we done enough?" A learning leader's role is demanding; it requires insight, strength, and perseverance for the organization to be successful. It is often said, "You cannot be a leader or a manager without followers." So, if you look around and you are alone, something is seriously wrong.

> **The question you should continue to ask is, "What more can we do?" It is never, "Have we done enough?"**

Increase your knowledge base and use it to develop employees. Continually gather information from your competition. Find out what other communities use for technology, systems, and engagement practices. Keep an eye on emerging products and services. Study your competition and incorporate applicable ideas into your community.

Ask yourself:

- Can I honestly say that I spend time each week learning what our competitors are up to?
- Have I picked up any new information?
- Have I incorporated learnings into my community?
- Has our team improved on them?

Leaders are readers—be on the lookout for information that will make an impact on your community. Share the information you gathered with your staff, and encourage them to do the same. Tell them to keep their ears and eyes open for new ideas and encourage them to bring those ideas back to the community. If you want your staff of stars to stay on your starship, you need them to feel they are engaged in the creation of the best galaxy in the universe—your community.

Have you ever been excited and highly engaged in a topic at a professional development seminar that your organization held, which included top managers and company officers, only to look around and see the president of the company on his phone?

This happened during a seminar I attended. At first, I thought the president had to answer an important email and was briefly distracted. However, 20 minutes later, when he was still glued to his phone, I became annoyed. I figured something was obviously more important to him than actively taking part in the seminar. After all, we had flown for many hours to attend this seminar (which we were required to attend), so we thought the subject matter was critical.

When we began our presentations, and the first manager spoke on a topic that she had gone great lengths to prepare, I looked back to see if the president had finally put down his phone. To my astonishment, he was gone. Not only had he left the room, but he didn't even say "good-bye"!

I had a great deal of respect for him before this incident, but as soon as I realized that we weren't important enough to receive so much as a "thank-you" or a "good-bye," my opinion of him plummeted.

If you are going to set the expectations for others to follow, you must set the example. This showed a total disrespect for our time and efforts, as people and as professionals. If you are going to show up, be present.

Chapter 10

Keep an Open-Door Policy

Keep an open-door policy and be available. This single act
sends a positive message to the entire organization. You will be
regarded as approachable with the desire to be available to
anyone who needs support or guidance. This is especially
comforting to those frontline workers who deal with day-to-day
events resulting from all sorts of residents' issues.

*It was late one afternoon, and I was in my office reading and
responding to emails. I could hear voices escalating just outside the office
area in the hallway. I could hear a back-and-forth conversation that was
spiraling out of control. A man's voice got louder and louder. Just as I
made the decision to jump up from my desk and deal with it, a staff
member who happened to be walking by the incident came running into my*

office. He informed me that Mr. Hothead was screaming in the office assistant's face and would not back down.

I didn't stop to listen, but asked him to walk with me and tell me what he saw. As he filled me in, I reached the altercation. The office assistant was reduced to tears, which made me furious. But my job is to de-escalate situations for everyone's best interest, and adding my fury would offer no solution. I firmly asked the resident to follow me, removed him from the area, and dealt with him in my office.

If I had my office door closed, I would not have heard this altercation, and things could have taken on an even worse turn for my staff. I do not respond to every loud or angry resident for fear that the staff member dealing with the issue will feel less than capable if I come charging to the rescue each time I hear loud voices. But there is a point at which my inner wisdom causes me to respond, and my staff has never once said they have regretted that I jumped in the middle of one of these situations. They have even gone so far as to thank me for my support and for being there to help.

In every business, there are times when a resident or customer is out of line and needs a heavy hand. As a leader, being available and responsive creates an atmosphere of trust and safety and keeps employees feeling cared for and supported. An open-door policy is useful and helpful and offers many advantages. It also shows residents that you are "in the building and ready at the helm." This sends a clear message: Someone is in charge and available for emergencies. It's all good!

In addition to being available to handle a crisis, your open-door policy encourages real-time dialogue between you and your staff. This has many advantages, which includes friendly exchanges and allows your employees to seek help quickly rather than sit on pressing issues. The main challenge of the open-door policy is that it can be terribly disruptive. However, the benefits outweigh the challenges. You want staff to know you are there for them and will be responsive if need be. It is critical for your staff and residents to know you are available and part of the team.

The open-door policy works both ways. It not only allows employees and colleagues to slip into your office, it also allows you to slip out. Wander around the community and get a feel for what is going on in real time. This is so important that if you can't remember to do it naturally throughout the week, schedule time in your calendar. This wandering around allows you to touch base with employees and residents. It shouts out, "I am here; this community is important to me and so are you. I want to know what is going on, and I want to see our employees because they are important to say hello to and to check in to see how their day is going."

If there is one action you can take to send a positive message, it is the act of wandering. You cannot manage behind a desk; you can't get a handle on what is really going on in the community from behind your desk. Regularly get out of your office to see, hear, and feel what is going on in the community.

Your presence as you walk around, stopping to talk, should not be a sighting as rare as a lunar eclipse. Show you are part of the fabric of the community, part of the team that is present every day. You are not someone who sits on a pedestal behind the large desk in the corner office sending a hierarchal message that says, "I'm too busy to come out. My work is more important than seeing you and saying hello." Walk around the community and adjust pictures on the wall that look as if motion has tipped them off-center and pick up something off the floor that someone has dropped or passed by—any excuse will do.

You care about the community, so show yourself and bring a smile to your employees' day. Check in with them, find out how they are doing, and ask about their family. This process is called rounding. Doctors perform this as a matter of course to check on their patients; they refer to it as "making the rounds." You need to do the same thing—check on your employees. You may not be a doctor, but when you stop to speak with staff members, give them a shot of encouragement. Be present when they speak; be encouraging of the work they are doing; believe they can handle whatever task they are faced with; thank them for a job well done and blow them away with kindness and respect.

When employees see you on a regular basis, you become one of them. They see you as a peer, not

They see you as a peer, not soaring above them.

soaring above them. You are building relationships, and you are learning about what makes them tick. However, you need to prepare yourself because you will eventually hear more than you bargained for. Employees will develop a great sense of trust and begin to share all sorts of information. Some of this will be personal; you will hear stories about their weekend, their families and a lot of information that might even surprise you. But, just as important, you will learn how trainings have been received, what is working, and what isn't—information that will help you to improve the community culture and keep employees engaged. This feedback is priceless, and you never would have heard it sitting behind your desk. Wander today; wander every day.

Chapter 11

Communicate Expectations

Communicate high expectations

Set specific goals in detail to give your employees something to reach for. Write them down and discuss them. Explain the importance of their role as it relates to the organization's mission and strategies. Be clear that you expect something above and beyond how other communities perform. Let them know you are building the community with stars, and you feel everyone has that potential.

Communicate clear expectations.

Be specific—make sure there is no vagueness about what you expect. For example, we expect employees to pitch in when they see an additional hand is needed. There should be no confusion in anyone's mind about what is expected of them. You are expecting excellence, so set the bar high and let them know what that looks like.

Communicate expectations at every level.

Emphasize and repeat your expectations consistently to staff consistently and at every level. When you spend time with employees, re-affirm your belief in their extraordinary capabilities. Make each contact with them count. Reinforce expectations consistently, formally, and informally.

It is critical that you have discussions early on and that are ongoing about what is expected of them in their position. It is your responsibility to ensure that you are clearly spelling out what is expected from both you and the organization.

Chapter 12

Ask Tough Questions and Listen

Crucial to learning and engaging your organization is the ability to ask questions and encourage the same. Do not pretend that you know everything. When you appear all-knowing, it's difficult to keep the respect of your employees. It is better to be known for your insatiable

It is better to be known for your insatiable passion for learning than to be known as a know-it-all, which you are not.

passion for learning than to be known as a know-it-all, which you are not. Leaders who admit their own shortcomings command greater loyalty and respect. Those who pretend they are gods eventually are exposed. You don't need to have all the answers; instead, you need to show good judgment.

When you ask questions of employees from all levels of the organization, you help bring realistic, bottom-line answers to the surface. Some responses may be difficult for you to hear, but

> **The question you should continue to ask is, "What more can we do?" It is never, "Have we done enough?"**

encourage this kind of honesty and truthfulness. Honest exchanges promote a sense of respect and trust in relationships; it's the willingness to listen that opens the channels in the mind. Tap into staff members who think differently. Diversity of ideas is what creates a fantastic landscape for discovering and uncovering unique thinking. A lack of diversity of ideas leads to a race to the bottom. People make decisions based on what they value, so by asking questions of a highly diverse group of people, you are going to get very different answers. Strive to open minds and discuss everyone's ideas.

Ask questions during your team meetings and have your employees write down their answers anonymously. Collect the ideas, and you will find that regardless of how well the group works and thinks together, you will get very different ideas from everyone. Go for it.

I conducted workshops for several major Boston area hospitals many years ago and had the privilege to teach what they called at the time, "teams and service" workshops. Without receiving any lesson plans, expectations, or guidance on what to teach, I had piles of worksheets to use on what I thought they wanted from me. They gave me full reign over what approach I wanted to take, so I came prepared to teach the typical topics on customer service.

When I walked into the silent classroom, I was shocked. What I saw stopped me in my tracks. The classroom consisted of a highly diverse group of people with varied socio-economic backgrounds. In addition, they were sitting on opposite sides of the room. Similar to grade school, where boys sat on one side and girls sat on the other, I found two very distinct clusters of people sitting apart. But this was a different kind of divide—these were adults. Scanning the room, the students looked anxious and awkward. There was an obvious divide; it was horrible.

I immediately asked everyone to arrange their seats in a circle, primarily so they could all feel connected and could see each other when they spoke. I asked people to introduce themselves, share their names, where they were born, etc., and I tried something different to attempt to break down the walls. I asked them to tell us why they worked in resident care; what they couldn't live without; and if they had a million dollars, what would they do with it. (This always ends the exercise with laughter, dreams, and happy thoughts, which we needed badly).

After we went around the room, and they began to feel more alike than dissimilar, I started a discussion on how people make decisions about what they value. We began to talk about the meaning of service and how that translates into taking care of people as well as how that affects them on a personal level in their day-to-day work. What started out as a quiet,

75

anxious collection of individuals, soon turned into a cohesive classroom of people who were actually nodding and agreeing with one another. They seemed to realize they were all committed to their work regardless of their color or language challenges.

I could see and feel the room shifting from stressed to calm and realized that was the work I had to do. Suddenly, a large man about 40 years old began to cry. The room went silent. I didn't know what to do, but knew I had to do something. So, I asked him calmly if he was all right or if he needed to leave. He pulled his hands away from his wet his face and told us the day before a resident had passed away while he was feeding her lunch. He told us that he loved the older woman like a mother.

Then something amazing happened. A woman stood up from her chair, crossed the room, and walked over to this man. She stood in front of him, placed her hand on his shoulder, and said, "She knows you love her. You left a piece of yourself with her, and when she left, she took it. She has that with her now, and you have a piece of her. You are a good man." He looked up at her and took her hand from his shoulder and held it, smiled, and thanked her.

I wanted to bring this group together. I wanted each person to walk away knowing how important his or her work is, and that our mission is a shared one. But that kind woman did

Answers and lessons come from the most unpredictable places. Open the dialogue and listen.

more for the class that day than I ever could. With a few short steps, she crossed the chasm and connected them through a single act of compassion.

76

Answers and lessons come from the most unpredictable places. Open the dialogue and listen.

★ Remind your staff that it is everyone's uniqueness that makes them a better team. Encourage honesty. Get candid about what is really going on and have those discussions. Tough issues often act as glue to connect us and strengthen our ties to one another.

★ Look employees directly in the eye, tell them you value their ideas, and then ask their opinions. This single act may be something that no one has ever done with them before. Be the first.

Chapter 13

Provide Continuous Feedback

Provide ongoing feedback. Informal feedback is a terrific learning tool and is a helpful way to learn about how you are doing and what you can do better. Be prepared—you can expect to give and receive more feedback from the emerging demographic of Millennials than any generation before them. The speed at which they communicate with one another through texting and social media has trained them to expect to hear back quickly and effortlessly. But the workplace is not a social application. For feedback to be communicated effectively and received openly, it is best when it follows a set of rules so it doesn't create walls or damage motivation. The elements of constructive feedback below are crucial for it to be successful.

First, feedback must be timely.

Timeliness is important for a couple of reasons. To gain the most from feedback, it has to be communicated as soon as possible. Then move on. This allows staff to gain insight to make necessary changes and learn from it. The benefit of timely and desired feedback accelerates the learning cycle. Once you provide feedback, the team can more readily identify problems and can learn from and implement changes quickly. You must

---

Welcomed feedback is feedback well received.

---

regain momentum and re-engage —with constructive criticism —for optimum learning. Timing of feedback is critical.

Second, staff must want to hear the feedback.

Uninvited feedback can feel like negativity and criticism if it is not received in the spirit in which it was meant. When giving feedback to employees, let them know you have observed them and ask them if they want to hear feedback on what you've observed. If they say no, respect that this may not be the best time for them to hear it. But let them know that you have feedback you need to share with them, and it is critical for their growth and development. Give them a few days to come back to you, but don't be surprised if that employee shows up in your office before the end of the day. The employee may be aware of the issue, and need time to get prepared to discuss it. If they don't come to see you in the next few days, reach out to them and set up a meeting to get it done. Welcomed feedback is feedback well received.

Last, do it in private.
Step into a safe and private environment, free of distractions and away from others who might be able to hear this critical exchange.

> **Provide negative feedback in a private setting and positive feedback publicly.**

This is the most effective environment. Provide negative feedback in a private setting and positive feedback publicly.

Teach the elements of giving and receiving feedback to your managers. Make it part of the culture. You are all about learning and engaging your staff's hearts and minds. While communication is a core principle, the receiver must welcome it.

Feedback is also instrumental in uncovering the many blind spots that lie within the framework of a person's character. Blind spots—habits and expressions, which may not be obvious to us but are very obvious to others—are parts of our personalities. Feedback turns the light on these blind spots and can provide powerful markers along the learning journey.

I remember after I learned the concept of how to give and receive feedback and its effects, I wanted to try it with a coworker. Keep in mind, the coworker was nervous about how this would play out. After all, it was my idea, not his. Since one of the rules is, "you have to want to hear feedback," I wasn't so sure that he was as committed to it as I was. I asked if he would begin by giving me feedback on what might be one of my blind spots. I asked him to be brutally honest and tell me something that I may not know about myself that would help me grow.

He just looked at me for a few seconds and finally said, "You have a unique way to make people feel better immediately." I remember laughing my head off at this. I thought he would tell me something negative, but here he was saying something positive. I realized that I associated the word feedback with negativity. So, after I stopped laughing, we spent the next few minutes giving each other positive feedback. That's when it struck me— positive feedback is still feedback, and it did help me to learn about myself through his eyes.

Consider setting up an online feedback forum; call it PFIG (Positive Feedback Is Great), a forum where employees can anonymously request or submit feedback at any time. Again, negative feedback is best expressed privately. For this positive feedback to make an impact and create an engaged and supportive culture, set it up so all staff can access it and contribute to it. Talk about transparency!

Chapter 14

Learn from Mistakes

In an engaging, learning organization it is OK to make mistakes while taking risks. It is *not OK* to avoid risk-taking and expect to do better. When faced with an employee or an idea that didn't turn out so well, make sure you communicate that mistakes are our best teachers. Great lessons come from risk-taking. Remind your staff, "We are in it to win it, so let's keep learning, and we'll get it right the next time." Be their cheerleader.

> **Great lessons come from risk-taking. Remind your staff, "We are in it to win it, so let's keep learning, and we'll get it right the next time."**

Caring for a senior living community is not just about resident care; it is also about taking care of the building, and keeping it safe, warm, and operational.

One day, a maintenance tech told me that one of the residents had a problem in his unit with the ceiling fan. It was making a really loud vibrating noise when the blades spun. He asked if he could switch it with a quieter fan in the room of a resident who was hard of hearing. I told him he couldn't because his suggestion was unethical. I asked him to go back into the resident's room, take a picture with his phone of the make and model number, and to order a new one. So, off he went.

The next day, the resident with the noisy fan came into my office shaking and very angry. He shouted, "Why did you install a $10 fan in my room? We pay thousands of dollars each month for these apartments!"

I was stunned. "Where was he getting this information?" I wondered. I assured him that it was not a $10 fan. But he was adamant and told me that the electrician said so. I was even more confused. I told the resident I would get to the bottom of it and get back to him that day.

I called in my maintenance tech and asked him what happened. My tech explained that after he left my office he went to the resident's apartment and took a picture of the fan. While he was chatting with the resident, he texted the photo to our electrician. The electrician texted back right away that the fans were cheap and not to bother him over a $10 motor. Then my tech told me that he showed the resident the text from the electrician. I asked him why he did that, and he said he liked the resident a lot and thought it would be helpful for him to see the electrician's response.

*I knew many managers would really lose it over his poor judgment.
Instead, I told him how upset the resident was and asked him if he thinks
it is a good idea to share information meant for him with residents—and
more importantly, if he would do that again. Embarrassed, the
maintenance tech said, "No, I get it. I get very close to these residents
because I am helping them all day, but business is business, and I really
shouldn't mix up the two."*

What a great lesson—on many levels. It is difficult to keep
business and personal relationships separate when working with
residents day in and day out. Personal relationships develop,
and it is challenging to maintain a professional distance. I told
the tech I agreed with him. Sometimes it is difficult to separate
feelings from good judgment. This technician was one of our
best, and it was worth helping him learn from his mistake. As a
bonus, our working relationship strengthened by the sheer fact
that I sought to understand him rather than punish him for that
decision.

Never dismiss an opportunity to develop your staff,
especially if it originates from a hard lesson. Some feedback can
wait, and some feedback cannot. This feedback and the
discussion about how he needs to handle himself with residents
were an important part of the discussion with him. Timing is of
the essence and especially important for employees who are just
starting out or finding the learning curve steep and wide. And
just as important, say what must be said, and then let it go.
Least said, soonest mended.

✦ Next time a member of your team makes a mistake, remind the employee that an important characteristic of a learning organization is making honest mistakes. The goal is to learn from them and to avoid repeating the error. Nothing smothers innovation faster than imposing fear or punishment on those who came up with ideas that turned out to be flops. Fear stifles creativity, which is the opposite of the kind of community you want to build. Send the employee back to work saying, "I can't wait to see what you might come up with next time, and I have full confidence in you to take a different approach and continue to find a better solution."

✦ If the employee still feels badly about the error (assuming it didn't harm anyone), try this: Pull out a pencil with a worn eraser. Hold it up, point to the worn-down eraser and say, "Mistakes are what erasers are for, and we all make them."

Chapter 15

Share Information Rapidly

There is value in learning information quickly, and there is risk in being uninformed and vulnerable to missed opportunities that could move the community ahead. A successful organization creates avenues that allow information to flow with speed, honesty, and openness. It is at the heart of the organization's ability to act swiftly and astutely. It is important to take a good hard look at your community's learning highway, noting its flaws and attributes.

Try these approaches for seeking information *inside* your organization:

1. **Know who you are.**
   Self-knowledge is fundamental for learning organizations.

Ask for feedback often. By equalizing the power between you and your employees, you can gather more accurate information—what's really going on versus what you hope might be going on. Jim Collins, the author of *Good to Great*, writes about how "good is the enemy of great." In a learning organization, you are leading the charge by constantly calibrating yourself and the community to the highest standards. Schedule this process regularly in your calendar with what I call "*stop and ask*" and ask yourself the following questions:

- How well do I understand the issues facing the industry?
- How well do I understand the issues facing our employees?
- How well do I stack up against other leaders in the industry's commitment and process as it relates to employee engagement?
- How good is our system for sharing information within the community?
- How well do we share ideas, celebrations, and milestones?
- How well do I know what makes my employees tick?

Can you answer these questions with "good" or "great"? Remember good is the enemy; strive for great.

2. **Share information freely throughout the organization.**
    Promote company-wide learning. Good internal
    communication requires transmitting and implementing
    ideas from one department in the community to another.
    Foster an environment where the team can share problems
    and solutions. Network across the whole community. Bring
    various departments together to compare notes and learn
    from each other. It is so interesting and disturbing that
    many communities don't utilize their own human resources
    for educational and training purposes. So much of what
    your employees do well can be shared and taught among
    departments. Reach out to the shining-star employees and
    ask them to provide a 15-minute exercise on something they
    do well. It can be a fun way for others to learn important
    skills from one of their own. Hiring outside trainers can be
    instrumental in addressing fundamental areas necessary for
    your staff's education, but you also have a wealth of talent
    in your own galaxy. Let them shine.

Using plain white paper, cut out a large shape that
resembles a light bulb. Tape it above a doorway. Encourage
employees when standing under it to come up with a great idea.
It can be about anything: celebrating a new holiday, a new
event, an idea that they have been kicking around. Similar to the
way people react to mistletoe, you will have those employees
who love to stand under it, and others who avoid it. Try it; it's
all in good fun.

3. **Avoid hoarding information for personal power.**
   Communicate a clear message that your commitment to
   learning is for the good of the entire community, not for
   individual gain. Create cultural norms that place a high value
   on honesty, even in the face of difficulty. Create an
   atmosphere where problems can be visible so that you and
   your team can find solutions quickly.

Chapter 16

Good Ideas Come from Everywhere

The best organizations spend little time trying to adapt an old solution to fit a new problem. An engaged learning environment places a high value on creativity and risk-taking elements of the organization's culture. One of

> **The best organizations spend little time trying to adapt an old solution to fit a new problem.**

the worst energy vampire statements that can instantly kill motivation (and a personal irritation of mine) is, "…but we've always done it that way." Set the tone by embracing novel approaches and new ideas. Experiment. Face issues with fresh eyes and see problem-solving as a genuine learning opportunity. Run ideas by objective people in different departments.

Numerous catalysts exist to spark creativity. You can drive it by recognizing the performance gap between the organization's current position and where it needs to be. Employee requirements or residents' needs, etc. can trigger creativity. Whatever the source, use the catalysts to keep the wheel of learning in motion.

Jeanette managed an assisted living community and felt lucky to have a fantastic office assistant to support her as well as oversee collections. The property was a very large one with over 1,000 residents, and the rents were controlled by the CPI (consumer price index). Because of this control, they needed to be diligent in their rent collection duties and to pay all the bills for the property. In other words, raising rents was not an option; therefore, collections were a high priority.

She understood that with the aging population, residents faced many health issues, which only compounded over time. Some of the issues were early onset dementia and other age-related conditions. Frequent doctor appointments and related activities often resulted in late or missed rent payments. Jeanette asked her assistant if she had any creative ideas on how best to deal with the problem.

Her assistant came up with a few great ideas. One idea was to offer to drive to the resident's home (which was easy to do since the business office was situated in the center of the homes on the property) and pick up their check to save them a trip to the office. Another idea she had was to send residents who were continually late a personal note and include the automatic payment form. This had never been done before, but it was worth a try. Later, we learned that this property had never been able to collect 100 percent of the rent payments.

After several months of diligently sending out the notes and the forms, Jeanette's assistant did it! She collected 100 percent of the rents for that month. The corporate office was shocked and, of course, extremely happy. But what amazed Jeanette was the pride the assistant felt in her accomplishment. After the woman left for the evening, Jeanette printed a congratulatory certificate and taped it to her assistant's computer so that when she came to work the next day, it was the first thing she saw. Jeanette had also come to know her assistant well and understood that she has a hard time coming in on Mondays, especially after a great beach weekend. So, Jeanette gave her the following Monday off with pay.

The assistant is an obvious star employee, and her commitment to success and thinking up new ideas is nothing less than stellar.

Include and encourage employees to develop imaginative solutions and new ways of thinking about situations, problems, and opportunities. Then implement the best ideas, regardless of their origins. To foster high engagement, ask all team members to contribute their thoughts and ideas. It sends a message of trust and belief in their contributions and creates engagement by allowing them to feel they have made an important contribution—they helped build the best galaxy in the universe. They are stars. Those good feelings make it difficult for team members to leave.

Professional development is often the main reason people want to work for certain companies, especially for the unskilled worker. Bring in thought leaders at regular intervals to present relevant topics and lead applicable discussions, facilitate professional development topics, and encourage continuing education. Budget for this and make it part of your culture. Be a resource for your staff and communicate your openness to discuss any issues that challenge and motivate them to learn more. Change your organization from a team of passive employees to aggressive learners.

The graph below shows the "Idea Triangle" as an ongoing process. The ideas go somewhere; they have direction, and they flow with connectivity.

Ideas should come from everywhere. Encourage employees to continually look for ways to improve on the status quo and ask them to bring ideas back to share with the team. Praise and reward employees for their ideas and, most importantly, celebrate them. Show your staff you value their contributions and that they matter.

Unfortunately, for many employees, active learning is beyond their interest or desire. Some employees are perfectly happy to come to work, do their job with minimal effort, and punch out. They choose to go along for the ride rather than be part of the team that steers the starship. However, some of those passive employees may eventually get motivated once they understand the value of it by seeing the excitement in others. You need to champion that. Emphasize the importance of learning and reward active learners; build your team with "shining stars." Take time to read what other communities are doing; for example, what they're using for technology and other best practices. Make the rounds at your facility and visit with your residents as well as colleagues at other communities. Ask questions, network, and always keep an eye and an ear open for new and exciting ideas.

Post successful ideas on the lunchroom bulletin board. Give the board a fun title, such as "Shoot for the Moon" or "Reach for the Stars."

Pin a large board, colored in deep sky blue, on the wall. Cut out several big yellow stars from construction paper, write employees' great ideas on the stars and post them.

Continue to add stars until the board is full of stellar ideas. Post employees' ideas on the community website, in the newsletter, etc. Communicate their ideas on every level and in highly visible places. Give recognition to the team by broadcasting their ideas.

People are naturally curious. They're just grown-up kids after all. But the work is important, not childish. Introduce a formal program of continuing education. Gather your team monthly for "Wisdom Circles" to share learning and discuss ways to do things better. Assign them research work. Ask them to investigate what other communities are doing and to bring their discoveries back for discussion during these meetings. Then put this learning into action. Don't stop there—invite residents into your Wisdom Circles and get their input on products and services.

At an assisted living community several years ago, the residents had a growing demand for van rides to their doctor appointments. Management saw this as an annoyance, and these demands did not fall into their current schedule. So, after a long discussion with the residents and the staff, they decided to try a new schedule. The community would provide a bus that traveled south one day a week and north on a different day of the week. This allowed residents to make their appointments based on the new bus schedule. What started out as a problem turned out to be a godsend for the residents. This wouldn't have happened if the managers had remained stuck in their thinking. Once they stopped, examined the problem, and sought out ideas, a perfect solution resulted. The families were thrilled since they often had a difficult time leaving work to get their loved one to an appointment, and the residents felt more independent and relieved they could get to the care they needed without depending on their family members.

Ask your caregivers to sit each week with a different resident for a 20-minute, one-on-one chat over a cup of coffee. Buy old-fashioned butter cookies or a dessert that might bring them back to the days when they had nice chats with neighbors. Ask the caregivers to get to know the residents individually; for example, ask where they are from, how many kids in their family, what they did for work before they retired, where they summered, etc. The caregivers will also talk a little about themselves. Then, during the caregivers' weekly meeting, ask them to share the information they gathered about each resident.

You won't believe how effective this is in helping the caregivers to see the residents as individuals rather than patients/clients. They will be surprised at what they and the residents learn about each other and how that translates into higher-quality care. This effort brings forth information for better resident-staff communications and creates a more engaged environment because close relationships begin to develop. Through the course of these meetings, as caregivers begin to share information about residents, their coworkers will pipe in and add what they know.

The information-sharing process leads to healthy discussions. Through intelligent dialogue, practical ways for improving care will naturally surface. When you gather an engaged group of likeminded people, who offer

They see them as an extended family, and they take comfort in that and feel committed to make their residents' lives more comfortable

support to each other, they learn together and develop the same goals. This tactic leads to quality care because they have a better understanding of the resident as an individual. If caregivers feel close to the residents they care for, they can't imagine leaving them. They see them as an extended family, and they take comfort in that and feel committed to making their residents' lives more comfortable. That is important work; it is care on a higher level, which results in a closeness that makes it very difficult for employees to leave.

When dealing with a problem facing the community, share it with your staff. Then ask them, "What's great about this?" Since looking at a problem or negative event can create a defeatist outlook, ask this question and shift their thinking. Your goal is to open their minds to thinking beyond the pessimism that problems create and encourage them to work toward a positive outcome. Remind them of the important work they do, and how everyone's efforts affect the bottom line. Reiterate your commitment to support them and not let them down.

Many years ago, I was working with a few employees on a new project initiative that higher-ups dropped into our laps. It had no clear mission except to provide the best customer service we could. So, we set up a basic system to take calls and respond to them. We had been moving along, tackling the everyday issues without any major problems. However, one day a high-level executive called me. He was upset and confused about our approach to one part of the project. The employees listened on the conference call in silence. When the call was over, they were devastated and afraid of losing their jobs. I reassured them that we would straighten it out and not to worry because I knew we would rectify the situation. But the mood was low. So, I asked the question, "Ok, what's great about this?" My staff just stared at me like I had a screw loose, but I just sat there and stayed very quiet for several minutes. Then suddenly, a bright member of the team said, "Well, maybe it will force corporate to communicate exactly what they are looking for rather than let us operate in the dark."

I was proud of this employee. This was a great point. Give employees a chance to rise to the occasion without always filling in the blanks for them. Through the

Give employees a chance to rise to the occasion without always filling in the blanks for them.

process of encouraging them to seek answers, you guide them

to think independently. Sometimes it may feel as though there are no perfect answers, but by encouraging employees to develop and use their critical thinking skills and good judgment, you will help them create a strong platform to make good decisions. This results in improved employee performance. By lighting sparks of engagement, you let them know they make a difference.

When the group makes a decision, and puts it into action, it has the natural tendency to bring your team together. Debrief the results with them in an "After Action Review" (AAR), and ask the following questions:

1. What actually happened?
2. What was supposed to happen?
3. What was the difference?
4. What should we continue to do?
5. What should we do differently? (This question is powerful.)
6. Act. Put some part of that decision in place immediately.

Most people or organizations don't ask the first two questions. If you really want to experience groundbreaking learning and create an impact, then the answer is *experimentation*. Experimentation is radically new and different, but you need to answer the first two questions if you want to learn. AARs will help your team explore new territory. Use experimentation, take risks, and encourage critical thinking.

This exercise will begin
to teach staff to consider
the results while fine-tuning
the actions to take. To
create unity and
collaboration, engage staff

Employees learn best when they learn about one another while learning from one another.

in learning activities through interaction and focusing on
common goals. Employees learn best when they learn about
one another while learning from one another. You are asking
them to think, not just perform their jobs by rote. They will feel
vital and significant, and you will see your stars sparkling with
excitement when they begin to acknowledge that they are
making a difference.

When valuable ideas or suggestions come from employees,
encourage them to act. Tell them, "Try it out and let me know
how it goes." The key to organizational learning is to create a
relaxed, interactive environment where employees see how their
learning and actions affect the bottom line. It increases
employee motivation and keeps them involved and alert. When
you create an excited staff that is actively learning and engaged
in their work, it puts the community in an ideal position to hang
onto their shining stars—even in a candidate-driven job market.
Employees captivated by their work and a feeling of purpose
stay with organizations longer than disengaged ones.

I had the pleasure of meeting author David Gavin while I
was writing my thesis, and he relayed the following story to me.

I thought it was one of the most extraordinary examples of collective wisdom I had ever heard and asked his permission to include it in my thesis. He was most gracious to allow me to share it with any audience when I deemed it appropriate. Since that time, I have used it numerous times to illustrate the importance of working together to come up with workable solutions to seemingly impossible problems.

In the book, The Great Game of Business, author Jack Stack had an experience that illustrates the benefits of showing your employees that you're human and don't have all the answers. He shares his fantastic story of an incident at Melrose Park out in the Midwest. Truckers went on strike and shut down the highways. The company could not get steel delivered from the U.S. Steel plant in Indiana because snipers were shooting at the trucks. The company needed steel to build its tractors. If it didn't get the steel, people would be sent home and not be paid.

Stack was in charge of getting the steel but didn't know how he could do it. So, he brought several of the employees together and told them he was really in a bind. He asked them, "How are we going to transport two tons of steel from Indiana to Illinois without being shot at?"

Someone said, "School buses—they wouldn't shoot at school buses, would they?"

Another person said, "It depends who's driving the buses."

Someone else said, "They wouldn't shoot at nuns driving school buses."

That is exactly what they did. They rented a school bus and dressed the guys up as nuns. They picked up the steel, loaded it into the bus, and drove the bus back to Melrose Park. The solution came from everyone working together. Sharing the learning experience is a way of teaching each other.

This excerpt is a clear example of how effective it can be to collaborate with your staff when faced with an organizational challenge. It's smart business to gather and implement ideas from employees at all levels. It keeps everyone engaged and creates an atmosphere where the team wants to make a difference. Can you imagine the laughter coming from that bus when they arrived? Talk about building camaraderie while sharing an experience they'll remember for a lifetime. Retention develops when engagement is working.

Chapter 17

Use Laughter and Color

Incorporate humor into everyday activities. Have you ever been somewhere by yourself, and suddenly you hear boisterous laughter coming from the next room? Do you remember what happened next? You began to smile, right? You were also curious to see who was laughing and why. It is a fact—laughter is contagious, and it has the power to infect even the most negative souls. The great news is that is seems to play an important role in building strong bonds between people and strengthening relationships. It is also known to shift perspectives, allowing you to see situations in a more realistic, less stressful light. It infuses freshness into any situation and helps employees break out of ruts. Humor naturally draws people close together, which can have a significant effect on mental health. Humor creates a psychological connection, helps you relax and recharge, and keeps you from feeling overwhelmed. It's also a fabulous tool to help diffuse conflict.

Humor in the workplace can also help employees see the human side of business. People often confuse humor with bad jokes, sarcasm, or ridicule. That's not humor; that is destructive. However, properly used, humor can assist in building relationships among employees. I wonder if that fact was the basis for the ever popular "silly putty," but I digress.

Laugh at your own mistakes, and laugh with, not at, others when they make a mistake. Show employees that errors are a normal part of the learning process. When your staff has fun, they work more collaboratively, and every single day becomes a team-building activity. Laughter boosts productivity and forces an emotional connection. It breaks down barriers of diversity and encourages more honest communication—that is one powerful action. Laughter turns fun into serious business, and vice versa, so encourage it.

Early in my career, I taught second grade. The classroom was painted in bright colors, and the environment felt energized. Before classes started in the fall, the administration expected teachers to decorate classrooms, to create a fun and colorful atmosphere. We made vivid bulletin boards, hung cutouts of animals, machines, and other items of visual interest. When I went on to teach high school and then undergraduate students at various universities, I couldn't help but notice the walls were painted shades of "greige". I did not decorate my classrooms as I had done for younger children—but looking back, I realize I should have! Greige walls beget greige results.

The plain-Jane classrooms of higher education certainly *did not feel* like an energizing place to learn. Environment matters—the feeling needs to vibrate life and infuse energy. The physical space needs to be welcoming, warm, and bright, creating a workplace that screams, "Amazing and fun people work here!"

I was going through resumes one afternoon to fill a Certified Nursing Assistant (CNA) position for our memory care unit. If you have ever had the pleasure of filling this position, it is a daunting task. Finding that right person is a huge challenge due to the strict requirements, and we wanted a bright, calm, but energetic, person. We also needed someone experienced to work with our current CNA, Joan Roland, in a two-person team in a highly critical area. I came across what looked like a perfect candidate—highly skilled, great experience, and local to the community—a win! But then I looked at the applicant's name, and it was Joan Boland. When I read the name, I burst out laughing. My staff came running into my office with big smiles on their faces. They asked what was so funny. When I told them, they too burst out laughing and in unison said, "Hire her!"

It's a funny story, but a true one. What were the chances her name would be so similar to the current employee's name? It seemed absurd, and we found it hysterical. The laughter added a delightful and immediate shift in the mood. One moment we were focused on our work, and at the speed of lightning, we were unified through laughter. The mood stayed light for the rest of the day—talk about the power of humor.

Ask for volunteers to take turns being the CFO, the Chief Fun Officer, each month. Ask your CFO to look around at each department. Can changes be made to the work areas to bring a little fun into the workplace? If they can, make it happen.

Engage your staff by encouraging them to paint their work spaces and then ask their opinions on ways to create a more fun and engaging environment for residents. You may work in a facility that is shaped like a box, but it doesn't have to feel or look like one.

Take the concept of humor further and make laughter an early-morning event. Create a "happy hour" and serve juice with jokes. Ask a shining-star staff member to facilitate a group of residents to share corny and ridiculous jokes in a comfortable setting. Ask the employee to print a few jokes from the internet to warm up the group. You will be surprised how popular happy hour becomes and how fast it grows. Go around the room and ask the residents to take turns telling jokes or funny stories. When residents from other rooms hear the howling laughter, be prepared to put more chairs around the room.

⭐ Copy a funny comic strip as it relates to the industry in your "Leaders Corner" of the company newsletter. Add a joke, story, or message.

⭐ Smile as you walk around the community and watch others mimic you. Smiles are contagious, too, so exude a genuine smile and laugh at every opportunity. Communicate that humor is an integral part of your organization's culture.

In the movie Moonstruck, there is a scene with Loretta (Cher) and Ronnie (Nicolas Cage) that illustrates the power of humor. The scene takes place the morning after Loretta and Ronnie had been intimate for the first time. They met at Loretta's parents' home where they waited for Johnny (Danny Aiello), who just happens to be Ronnie's brother and Loretta's fiancé, to show up so they could break the news to him that they had fallen in love the night before.

As they waited, the mood became somber. Eventually, other family members entered the home and joined them for coffee. Loretta's grandfather was the last to come into the kitchen and sit down. He looked around the table feeling confused and worried over the expressions on their long faces. Suddenly, he choked out, "Somebody tell a joke!" He created an immediate comic relief, broke the gloom, and alleviated the stress in the room. It was a great scene—what a wise old man.

Laugh, smile, and joke around. Watch the power it has as it starts a ripple effect with employees and residents.

Chapter 18

Be Humble—Be Powerful

When we think of traits that leaders typically exhibit, we often
overlook one important component: humility. There is so much
talk about the power of influence and an over-confidence in
leaders, which is a very hierarchical style of leadership. This
attitude no longer fits the ideal collaborative model that
encourages an honest exchange of information necessary for
engaged communities. When you exhibit traits of humility, such
as requesting feedback and focusing on the desires of your staff,
it results in better employee engagement and job performance.
Being a humble leader is quite different than being overly
concerned with others' opinions or being an easy mark. It's
about being real and vulnerable, just like everyone else. People

want to work for those they see as human but can just as easily show decisiveness when the situation calls for it.

When employees believe their managers are genuinely looking out for them, team performance rises dramatically. That requires you to care about the environment in which your team is working and make sure they have the tools they need to do their job.

The best decisions often spring from a relaxed state of mind.

When you're willing to share your own mistakes and how you dealt with and recovered from them, you will earn your employees' trust. Own up to what you do because the message it sends is that you value honesty. Sometimes, you need to admit that you don't know the best answer and need to wait until you have better information to make a decision or a change. The act of waiting or weighing your thoughts and telling your team "to sleep on it" provides another important lesson to foster their learning process. Teach your team that time opens doors that may have been closed just days before. The best decisions often spring from a relaxed state of mind.

Use humility and state your expectations. Then get out of the way to let your employees do their jobs. It takes humility to admit that your way isn't the *only way* to get things done. Clearly, some people are better at certain aspects of a job than you are. Accept this and allow others' strengths to work for the good of the team without interference. Give positive feedback when you learn how an employee took a different course of action and landed with a great result.

Your role is to support your employees and to ask other managers to do the same with their teams. Your frontline people are the face of the organization, and they need to be supported, engaged, competent, and welcoming to the residents. Are you creating this type of organization with your vision and actions? Do your employees see you as a trusted supporter or a removed dictator? Turn your organizational chart upside down, and you gain humility. Begin to see your employees as stars, and keep them shining with the belief that you think *they are tops.*

An engaged and supported organizational chart

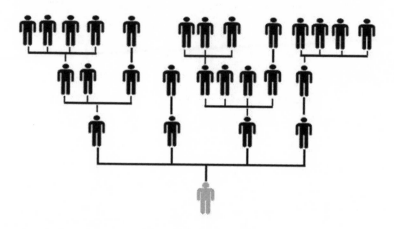

Does this organizational chart look strange? Look closely. It should look upside down because a typical organizational chart places the leader at the top—also known as top heavy. However, in an engaged learning organization, the leader sits at the bottom rather than on top. Leading in this direction creates a culture of support. Engagement is the byproduct of this support structure. It is the framework of solidarity and engagement. Take a second look. This is another reason the leader needs big shoulders!

Section III

A 90-Day Guide to Employee Engagement

Chapter 19

Onboarding

In the olden days (and from that reference you can probably surmise that I am not a Millennial), we used to call the process of training and acclimating a new employee an "orientation program." Since then, someone with great influence must have seen the workplace as a ship and changed the process to onboarding. But I must say, I like it. Onboarding feels right. It feels welcoming, as though someone is throwing you a line, and you are stepping aboard. It's as if they are saying, "You are one of us now. Come on board." And somehow, the term onboarding also makes the process sound more important than orientation does. The term orientation seems less formal and short-term.

Onboarding refers to a *process* of bringing new employees into an organization and preparing them to succeed in their position. It also socializes employees into the organization's culture. Effective onboarding helps employees understand their roles and how they fit into the organization. It implies they will be properly trained for their new role, equipping them with tools to gain the relevant skills and confidence required to make an impact within the community. Done effectively, onboarding should create a sense of pride among the employees about what the community stands for—its culture.

Successful onboarding is one of the most effective ways to bring about engagement in the senior living industry. Studies have shown that a well-executed onboarding program can turn a new hire into a happy and dedicated employee, decreasing the costs of turnover and creating a strong and thriving culture of cheerful workers.

Surely you can remember the anxiety and dread of that very first day you attended grade school. For some, it was filled with excitement, but for many, it was filled with fear. The first day on the job can bring similar feelings of anxiety, and new employees can feel just as vulnerable. Day one has the potential to make them feel awkward—from getting lost in the building to forgetting necessary paperwork. It is normal for new hires to be anxious and nervous on their first day in your organization.

But as stressful as starting a new job can be for the employee, it is no holiday for you—the manager—either. You have much to process, and it's often overwhelming to be responsible for making new people feel welcome, setting expectations, establishing their responsibilities, familiarizing them with the company culture, and at the same time, handling your own workload.

Unfortunately, not all managers are adept at executing this process or have the time it requires. If that's the case, this book is for you. You can rely on it as your *Engagement bible,* and you will be able to follow a simple, yet strategic, guide that will provide you with the best onboarding plan on the planet. It will engage your new hires and encourage them to feel like stars before they set foot in your community—yes, before they even show up. And the great news is that you can use this plan with any of your new hires, not only your critical caretakers.

The goal of the onboarding plan is not to leave your new employees alone to figure out the organization's culture and unwritten rules on their own. The last thing you want to do is to drop people into unfamiliar surroundings and leave them unsure where to turn for guidance. You don't want them wondering, "What should I do first? What are the expectations? Who will answer my questions?" If new hires feel alone, left to their own devices, and fearful of speaking up to ask questions, there is a very good chance they won't stick around, and they will jump ship.

Onboarding a new hire successfully in the first 90 days is crucial for both the individual and the organization, and it establishes a foundation for future success. The only way to ensure effective onboarding is to involve everyone and to make certain all employees understand the value of this process. "Everyone" includes all staff, management, and even the ever-important kitchen help. Onboarding must be part of the community's culture and belief system to be successful. The process is the engagement plan expressed in this book. You must put it into action. Make the process clear to all employees and set the expectations. For the engagement plan to work, you need an all-in commitment by the entire organization.

Communicate with clarity your expectation of support from everyone at every level. Let your employees know this plan is the organization's promise to help new people onboard successfully—and that it takes everyone's commitment and involvement. Tell them you are counting on each one of them to help the new employees succeed. Ask for their assistance. Tell them to provide feedback to management if they observe any concerning issues at any point within the first 90 days of an employee's arrival. Ask them to come forward and report their concerns as soon as possible to ensure the new hire's professional success and the community's best interest.

If you can onboard several new hires on the same day, that is ideal. You will see engagement take place right before your eyes. When onboarding several new hires at the same time, you have the fantastic opportunity to promote a dialogue that

A relaxed social setting acts like Super Glue; it connects people and helps to form relationships, which are fundamental for engagement. Use the Super Glue to link your stars.

identifies commonalities and shared interests among them. People naturally connect with familiarity, humor, and enjoyment. Take charge and connect those dots. Direct the conversations to give the new hires the chance to get to know each other. A relaxed social setting acts like Super Glue; it connects people and helps to form relationships, which are fundamental for engagement. Use the Super Glue to link your stars.

While introducing people to each other, ask them to share some personal information to jump-start a friendly conversation. When you facilitate a warm, inviting conversation, you create kinship right out of the gate. When new employees start, help them to make positive connections; this is crucial, especially on the first day and the first week of their employment. You won't know any personal issues they might be dealing with when they first come to work for you. But you do know they will thrive in a consistently supportive environment where they know someone is looking out for them. Help them make connections as soon as possible.

Chapter 20

Financial Investment for the First 90-Days

Real costs

Are you worried about what this 90-day engagement plan will cost? Well, let me ask you this: Do you want to

Do you want to budget for failure or plan for success?

budget for failure or plan for success? Let's do a simple review of costs you will incur if employees leave, including recruiting, hiring, and training.

Your current budget

It costs you approximately $3,000 a year to replace a $10.00 per hour employee.

It costs you approximately $30,000–$45,000 to replace a nurse or manager who makes $60,000 a year.

It costs you approximately $120,000 a year to replace a critical care nurse, or high-level director.

Current statistics reveal that approximately 40 percent of new employees leave within the first 90 days. So, what if you lose *several* new employees? Review the bullet points above and figure what it is going to cost you to go back to the drawing board and hire all new people.

Hanging on to your stars is priceless, and you'll be thrilled to learn it comes at a far lower cost than rampant turnover does. Now, let's look at the real costs of the 90-day onboarding plan.

Your plan for success

$40.00	New hire's onboarding gift.
$90.00	Engagement Coordinator's gift for the new hire's 90-day completion.
$90.00	New employee's 90-day gift.
$150.00	First-day lunch, including Hoodsies, for new hire and coworkers. If your community has a kitchen, costs could be less.
$14.99	A plant for the new hire's desk.
$40.00	Off-site lunch meeting with your star-to-be after 30 days.
$200.00	Reward for the Engagement Coordinator and all mentors.

$624.99	**Total** to ensure proper engagement of the new hire.

The approximate salary for the Engagement Coordinator is **$40,000,** depending on what additional duties are included.

It's simple math—invest in engagement to hang on to your stars.

Step 1

Choose an Engagement Coordinator to Light the Way

The first step the organization needs to take is to appoint an *Engagement Coordinator*. A dedicated person is necessary to spearhead, manage, and facilitate the initial 90-day engagement plan. I cannot emphasize more strongly the importance of this person. If you skip this step and do not put a person in place to light the way, close the book now because your engagement plan will fail. It is that simple. To engage new employees successfully during this critical first 90-day period, a devoted person coordinating the engagement plan is essential.

Some organizations think that their Human Resources department is responsible for the successful onboarding of new employees. It is implied that they will keep an eye out for any issues. But this is not what happens. Just ask any human resources professional. They have all they can do to manage and oversee many of the department's functions, including recruiting, hiring, managing payroll, and a myriad of other tasks. Tracking new employees takes someone with time and a flexible schedule who can take a hands-on approach.

Earlier we discussed the role of the CEO, the *Chief Engagement Officer*. This person leads the organization based on the established mission, values, goals, and objectives. The CEO is responsible for running the community and making sure engagement is always in action, but he or she is not able to take on the process of tracking new employees. Tracking and supporting new people will make the difference between successful engagement and failure to retain. The role of the Engagement Coordinator serves as the boots-on-the-ground professional who shepherds the new hires through their first 90 days. Since this person is the key to successfully implementing this guide, we will refer to our Engagement Coordinator for the ease of reading as *Ms. Keys*.

To give you a visual perspective, picture a room full of newly filled helium balloons. They fly throughout the room with all their beautiful colors. You can see them touch the ceiling and bounce off one another. Now leave the room, close and lock the door, and come back a week later. What do you see? The balloons are all drooping, yes? Some are lower than others, and most are on the floor. None of them are touching each other, and they are a sad-looking bunch.

During the first 90 days, the Engagement Coordinator (our Ms. Keys) acts as the helium that comes in contact with new hires and fills them up. From her first contact, she welcomes them with

During the first 90 days, the Engagement Coordinator (our Ms. Keys) acts as the helium that comes in contact with new hires and fills them up.

positive energy. Then she routinely contacts them and consistently refills them with strategic amounts of engagement deposits necessary to keep them fully engaged. The Engagement Coordinator is the new hires' guide, their go-to person, their friend, their rock of stability, their champion, a kind comrade, and a constant and available resource when they need someone familiar.

With all the activity that goes on in a senior living community, especially as the residents age and require more care, the community leader and the caretakers must persist in ready mode to respond to daily events they cannot predict. New hires deserve the time and effort it takes to get them onboard. Dedicating a competent person, an Engagement Coordinator, to see them through is essential and the key to success.

If costs concern you, and you don't want to budget for this dedicated person, you need to open your eyes. Sit down with your human resources director and comptroller and take a close look at the time devoted to recruitment and the endless costs of

turnover. Do you budget for turnover? Why would you budget
for a problem instead of an engagement solution? Make the
commitment to budget for this critical position. It will save
resources in the short term, and it's money in the bank in the
long term.

Their top priority and main responsibility is to successfully
onboard new employees, with suitable time in their schedule to
devote to the effort.

They are dedicated to the effort and held *accountable* for the
success of new employees.

Depending on the size of your organization or community,
it may require a full-time person to fill the position effectively.
Be highly selective of whom you choose, since the Engagement
Coordinator is the backbone and the lifeblood of the
onboarding plan. As such, this person will need your support
and ongoing dialogue as well as regular meetings with you and
the manager(s) involved with each new hire.

Engagement Coordinators keep notes on the new hires'
progress and concerns and look for ways to help them, whether
it's additional training or other effective methods you are using.
Trust her; she knows firsthand what is necessary. Help her get
the new hires what they need. Finally, the Engagement
Coordinator must report back to the new employees'
manager(s) to discuss progress and any concerning issues. Time
is of the essence. The sooner you resolve any issues, the more

successful the new hires will become. You have 90 days, and the clock is ticking.

When seeking candidates for the Engagement Coordinator position, look for a highly-organized person with excellent interpersonal skills, an easygoing personality and a warm nature. The ideal candidate smiles easily and genuinely enjoys helping people succeed. He or she must possess excellent follow-up and follow-through skills with the ability to methodically implement the specific tasks outlined in this 90-day guide.

This individual must be a natural "people person," love working with others, and feel personally committed to their success. You don't need a psychologist, but you do need to find someone with a keen insight into human behavior and a high level of emotional intelligence. If you don't have anyone on board with these skills for this important work, hire someone. You are looking for someone with the proper behavioral traits rather than someone with a perfect skill set. You can teach skills to just about anyone.

Often, community leaders do the work of the Engagement Coordinator if the community is *very small* and if they want to spearhead the engagement plan. But, if you want to commit to the strategy outlined in this guide, and you feel there is the slightest chance you will not be able to give your new employees the time it requires, you should not attempt to take on this role. If you do decide to take it on and then realize you are too busy to follow the guide, immediately put someone in place temporarily until you find the right person.

The best decision is not to try to be superhuman only to find yourself behaving more like an underdog. If you want your new hire to succeed, don't take a chance. Take this effort seriously, and don't gamble with time or resources. To be effective, the Engagement Coordinator must be actively involved in managing the day-to-day engagement plan and following each new hire.

Consistency is fundamental to the plan. This position requires singular, focused attention, flexibility, and availability, and it is not a good fit for a leader in high demand. With

For the success of this plan, a community needs a dedicated watchdog; new hires deserve the best chance they can get to succeed.

all the responsibilities and considerable effort required to run a community, I would **not** recommend leaders taking on this position, nor would I recommend a human resources employee attempting to serve in this role. For the success of this plan, a community needs a dedicated watchdog. New hires deserve the best chance they can get to succeed.

OK, so you've found the right candidate, and decided to hire Ms. Keys as your Engagement Coordinator. To begin, she will be your new employees' first contact. She will engage new hires from their first day and ensure they follow all the steps in the engagement plan. She will also involve key people to keep the engagement plan on course.

Ms. Keys will practice what I call "Velcro Management." This is not handholding; instead, the process involves management connecting with new hires and following them closely while providing input into their development. She will be a reliable and supportive resource for each new employee during his or her entire first 90 days—more so in the beginning and less so at the end when the new hire's supervisor joins in the engagement effort. But she will track the new employee throughout the first 90 days.

When the 90-days draws to a close, Ms. Keys will sign off on the completed plan and place it in the new hire's employee folder. The file will include documentation reflecting the person's progress, setbacks, and any notes on relevant issues. At the conclusion of the onboarding process, the new hire will acknowledge and sign off on a completion form that also goes in the file.

At the end of the 90-day plan, you will reward Ms. Keys. With the employee now happily engaged at the 90-day mark, present your Engagement Coordinator with a prepaid debit card for $90.00. Observing the new hire happily engaged is often rewarding enough, but use this gift to let Ms. Keys know that you appreciate her efforts and she has accomplished her mission. Tell her that she has star power, that she's a galaxy hero. This is significant when you think about the statistic that reveals over 40 percent of employees leave within the first 90 days. Celebrate her at the next managers' meeting and breathe a sigh of relief that you won't have to spend a bare minimum of $3,000 to recruit and train a replacement employee.

Understand, as successful as this plan will be, Ms. Keys may not *always* succeed at her task of retaining new hires. Sometimes new employees leave during the first 90 days for reasons organizations cannot know about or control. Ms. Keys should not be penalized for this, nor should she receive a reward. If a new hire leaves within the first 90 days, she will perform an exit interview. This will be done for any employee who jumps ship.

The exit interview not only offers insight into why new hires are leaving but also provides feedback on what they experienced in the community. If the employee speaks honestly, the information gathered may be useful to the organization to improve employee engagement practices. Exit interviews unearth a wealth of critical information. Take the time to perform this invaluable step, learn from it, and put the changes or lessons into action.

Exit interviews unearth a wealth of critical information. Take the time to perform this invaluable step, learn from it, and put the changes or lessons in action.

At the end of the book, you will find an excellent "Exit Interview" template with questions and techniques to help you capture the information you need to improve engagement. The feedback you receive from employees who have one leg overboard can be vital to your engagement plan.

Step 2

Start Early to Prepare the Galaxy

A successful engagement plan starts *before* the new hire's first day. Planning is the difference between success and failure. Plan as though

Let the plan be your guide.

guests are coming to your home and you want to make them as comfortable as possible. Let the plan be your guide. Below you will find a simple checklist to follow down to the smallest detail. Complete each step; the devil's in the details. You can add to this list but don't subtract.

The goal of this 90-day engagement plan is to create engaged, happy, shining stars-to-be. For the purposes of following along in this guide, let's give the new employee a gender and a name. Let's call him "Startobe" (star-to-be).

Once Ms. Keys has received the signed offer letter back from Startobe and has confirmation that he will be joining the team, it's *go time*. She will prepare his welcome package. Startobe is excited, so keep his head in the clouds and get this out to him immediately.

For the Engagement Coordinator

Include the following in the welcome package

- A personal, handwritten welcome note card with signatures from team members (or from his direct-report staff depending on the position) with whom he will be working.

- Any necessary paperwork *with instructions*, the dress code, employee handbook, and benefits information.

- The job description with the word "engagement" highlighted. This emphasizes that engagement is part of the job description as well as the expectation.

- A recent newsletter so Startobe can begin to read into the culture of the community.

- A monetary gift card for $40.00. The value amount will depend upon the position. Regardless of the position, provide this gift. Employees may need or want to make purchases for clothing, shoes, or some other job-related item.

- The first week's agenda so he will know what to expect.

- Any other related material for him to review prior to his first day.

Other steps to take

- Mail the package to Startobe.
- Email him and ask him to expect the package. Ask him to reply to your email when he receives it. You have begun the friendly communication process fundamental to the plan.
- Email his supervisor to confirm the welcome package was mailed and provide a copy of this checklist to inform the supervisor what Startobe will receive.

Order or gather the following

- Order business cards (if applicable).
- Gather any identification cards, keys, and security cards. If the identification card (ID) won't be ready, make a laminated paper one. You will require Startobe to wear his ID from his first day so employees can welcome him warmly using his name.

Five-to-seven days before arrival

- Review Startobe's schedule and make sure there is room for flexibility. Plan to follow the agenda, but don't let it obstruct you from switching from one activity to another if necessary to maintain momentum.

- Confirm all trainings with facilitators. Double-check room availability and schedule.

- Approach superstar employees who are truly inspiring, naturally kind, highly skilled, and positive and ask them to mentor Startobe. Some people love to teach, so encourage it. If the employee agrees, assign that staff member as a mentor for Startobe. Provide him or her with guidelines to follow to assure mentoring success.

- Set up a meeting with the mentor(s) and Startobe's supervisor. Review in detail the goals for the first 90 days. Make a list of all the duties, objectives to accomplish, and residents for whom Startobe will be accountable and then spread those goals over three months. Use the Outlook or similar calendar to schedule Startobe's individual plan.

- Make sure the employees who choose to be

Don't just hope for the best; work with the mentors to ensure their success.

mentors are clear about what is expected of them and the required timeframes for completion. The mentors may have good intentions, but don't assume they know how to translate their skills and knowledge to Startobe. Don't just hope for the best; work with the mentors to ensure their success.

Immediately below, you'll find mentoring parameters listed as "Mentoring 101." Discuss them in detail, since you don't want to leave mentoring to chance. These parameters are simple to follow and effective, so make it part of every new mentor's initiation.

Mentoring 101

Make sure you select qualified mentors. They must be intrinsically motivated, willing and able to devote the necessary time, and present themselves and the information positively. They need to be punctual and understand the importance of the following guidelines, which you will review with them in detail.

Instructions for the mentor

Start out slowly. Show Startobe the information slowly at first and then ramp up when you see he is making progress. New hires will show their speed and ability to grasp concepts at their learning pace. Forcing or pushing instruction does not work. If you do not see progress being made in a timely fashion, you will need to explain the importance of timeliness as it relates to that job or skill. If you notice that progress is taking far too much time, that skills are absent, or there may be a problem with learning, it's essential to seek out Ms. Keys to discuss further action.

Give thorough instructions. Effective instruction is based on a simple process that applies to most individuals. Ask Startobe to observe how a skill is performed, ask him to perform it, then ask him to show you how it's done. Train in steps throughout the process, ask Startobe if he has any questions. Keep communicating until you see Startobe becoming confident in his responsibilities. If some tasks are taking him longer than expected or are crucial to perform in a strategic order, write them down—whatever it takes to help him grasp the information.

Introduce the new hire into the culture of the community. Soft skills, including the ability to communicate with Startobe in a friendly way while explaining the culture's expectations and

Choose language that instills an understanding of what the community reveres as well as what it frowns upon.

values, are vital. Choose language that instills an understanding of what the community reveres as well as what it frowns upon. Share disastrous stories of past learning situations as well as those with happy endings to explain the mistakes and share in the enjoyment of positive outcomes.

Make sure you are aware of your own blind spots. Ask your supervisor to point out any blind spots you may possess that could hinder Startobe's learning. For example, if you tend to talk too fast when providing instruction, you need to understand this could cause big problems for Startobe. It impedes proper hearing, comprehension, communication, and learning—especially if there are any language challenges. Get feedback from your supervisor before you train Startobe. It may sound tough to ask for feedback, but not asking for it could result in ineffective instruction, frustration, and overall bad feelings between you and Startobe.

For the Engagement Coordinator

Reward successful mentoring. Reward mentors who successfully train Startobe to perform independently and effectively. Mentors are shining stars. Keep them happy in the community solar system so they will continue to produce positive energy. When Startobe completes his 90th day and becomes a contributing member of the community, offer mentors time off or a $90.00 gift card. Let them choose which one they would prefer.

Ask the team members working directly with Startobe to participate in a few team activities (below) to onboard and introduce Startobe to the team and the organization's culture. Buy the team lunch or set up bagels in the break room.

 Create a crossword puzzle

Ask the team to create a crossword puzzle. This is a great team-building exercise; it introduces the new hire to the community in an enjoyable and factual way. Ask them to brainstorm a list of people, departments, fun facts, and details about the community. Include key people's names, photos, dates, and trivia. There are many websites that offer simple designs and instructions on how to build a crossword puzzle. Visit this link to help you create a crossword puzzle: www.puzzle-maker.com.

On the next page, you'll find some possible clues to help you get started.

Keys to the Universe

Across:

4. In what room are the schedules kept?
6. What is the last name of your supervisor?
7. Whose photo is this?
8. We all make a difference every _ _ _.
9. The first-aid kit is kept in what room?

Down:

1. How many fire extinguishers are there on each floor?
2. Our primary goal is to provide the highest quality of
   _ _ _ _ for our residents.
3. What is the name of the executive director?
5. Thanks to you, what was the dessert we got to enjoy at
   lunch on your first day?
7. What is the name of your mentor's cat?

Answers

Ask your staff to make this puzzle simple and relevant, and to get it done. Once this is created, it can be used repeatedly, changing it only to update facts. This is fun but also a powerfully engaging way to introduce Startobe into the community. Make sure you ask questions that are important for him to know but throw in some silly questions, too. When Startobe begins searching for the answers to the puzzle, it will drive him to learn about his environment, accelerate his recognition of names and faces, and at the same time, get a feel for the culture of the community. Hand this blank crossword puzzle to him on the fourth or fifth day in his new position and ask him to complete it and return it to you in a few days. Make the crossword puzzle **simple, entertaining,** and **relevant.** The search for information will help jump-start the necessary connections in a fun and appealing way.

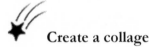 **Create a collage**

Instead of just handing Startobe the community's organizational chart with names and titles, create a collage with photos and personal information that includes the staff he will be working with. It could include photos of supervisors, co-workers, the Executive Director, and some information about their lives outside of work, such as family, pets, hobbies, travel destinations, favorite foods, etc.—whatever the employees feel comfortable sharing. With a smartphone and a color printer, you can put together a collage in a snap. It's a nice team-building activity, too. It lives up to its primary purpose and takes the pressure off Startobe to remember the many faces he meets over the course of the first few weeks. It puts a human face on the community and will make any newcomer feel like family. **Make sure you add his photo** to this collage once it's complete. It is a fun activity and it is a great engagement gift.

Three days before arrival

Ms. Keys will send a welcome email message to Startobe and copy his supervisor. It will include any missing or final new-hire forms for him to complete. On the next page, you will find an example of a simple, welcoming email.

Sample welcome email to Startobe

Subject Line: Welcome Aboard!

Dear Startobe,

It is my pleasure to welcome you to the Stars Community, and we are looking forward to seeing you on May 1. When you arrive, park in the back lot next to the ballfield, and I'll meet you at the main reception area at 8:00 a.m. As you know, Mrs. Meteor is your supervisor, but I get the pleasure of greeting you when you arrive.

We will provide lunch on your first day, so you have no need to brown bag it. 😊

We're looking forward to having you on board. Welcome to the team.

Warm regards,

Ms. Keys
Engagement Coordinator

cc: Mrs. Meteor, CEO/Executive Director, Human Resources

Complete the following tasks to ensure a welcoming atmosphere.

- Make sure Startobe's work area is empty and clean. Provide a new notebook, pens, and pencils—whatever he'll need for the week.
- Prepare a map of the building with departments clearly laid out, an employee directory, and a resident directory.
- If he will have a desk:
- Make sure his computer is working and that IT is available. Set up email and passwords and make sure to leave a written copy of phone instructions.
- Purchase a small, maintenance-free plant, such as a golden pothos, as a welcoming gesture and place it on his desk before he arrives.
- Place a small bowl of mints on the desk.
- If he won't be working at a desk, prepare an area or a private space where his personal items will call home. Make sure it is clean and that the previous person's name and belongings have been removed.

One day before arrival

Send an email to all the employees in the organization and announce Startobe's name, position, shift, and to whom he will be reporting. Encourage all employees to go out of their way to say "hello" and introduce themselves. Remind them to use Startobe's name whenever possible.

Sample email to send to staff

Subject Line: Please welcome Startobe aboard!

Dear everyone,

Great news! Please join me in welcoming our new employee, Startobe. He starts tomorrow morning and will be working directly for Mrs. Meteor. He lives in Pluto, and he has been working in the senior living industry for over five light-years. His mentors will be Saturn, Venus, and Mars. He is lucky to have you all to guide him under your excellence.

I get the pleasure of greeting him when he arrives, but please go out of your way to say "hello."

Lunch will be provided for those who will be joining us. Let me know today by 2:00 p.m. so I can order enough food. 😊

Thank you all in advance for engaging Startobe with all your great energy. He is joining one of the best communities in the universe.

Warm regards,

Ms. Keys
Engagement Coordinator

cc: Mrs. Meteor, CEO/Executive Director, Human Resources

You have only a few last-minute tasks to complete the day before Startobe's arrival.

- Check in with the mentors. Make sure they have the agenda and training schedule.
- At 2:30 p.m., order lunch to be delivered by 11:30 a.m. for Startobe and his mentors.
- Invite other employees to be present.
- Pick up several packages of Hoodsie Cups. Everyone loves a Hoodsie. It's a party, after all—a welcome party, so make it memorable. After lunch, pass out the Hoodsies, hold up the cups as if toasting Startobe, and welcome him to the team.

Step 3

Day 1: Welcome the Star-to-Be

Employees are either eager to dive in on the first day, nervous, or both. By handling most of the administrative tasks prior to their start date, you can keep their enthusiasm high. The first day should feel tension-free and exhibit order, giving Startobe a chance to follow along at a stress-free pace. With your Engagement Coordinator, Ms. Keys, in place, you are prepared and ready to create your star-to-be.

Day 1 agenda

First impressions count. Just as you would treat any guest in your home, you want to extend a warm greeting to Startobe.

- Be ready and waiting for Startobe at the main entrance door. Greet him with a big red-carpet "hello" and welcome him warmly as you would welcome your long-lost cousin you have not seen for years. (In some cases, this might be true if this position was difficult to fill.) Let him see your excitement as though you have been waiting for him for months.

- Make a note of the time Startobe arrived. This is important and telling. If he is early or on time, that's great; if he is late, this may be an indication of more tardiness to come. Ask him, "Did you hit traffic?" With any luck, Startobe will be forthcoming, apologize, and explain. But if he is late and does not provide a reason or apology, explain that it is important to be on time for his shift; often he is relieving a tired employee. Ask him if this will be a problem. Ask the tough questions now, and set the groundwork for expectations.

- Hand Startobe his ID/name badge. Explain that it is a protocol to wear it while on shift. (Make sure you are wearing yours.) Tell him that it is helpful for other employees to learn his name as soon as possible, and it makes the residents feel more comfortable, especially when he is caring for them.

- Make introductions as you pass other employees, residents, or clients. Make small talk if it feels natural, but don't force conversations.

- Take Startobe to his office or area that will hold his personal belongings.

Once his belongings are safely stored, introduce Startobe to his direct supervisor and talk a little about the day and what he can expect.

- When that meeting is over, take Startobe to the kitchen and bathroom area. Offer him a cup of coffee, tea, or water.

- Take this coffee break as an opportunity to review the first week's agenda together.

- Take his picture. He'll probably look his best on day one and not mind too much. Paste his photo in a document above his name and title to show the community he is a new employee. Set it prominently in the main reception area for all to see.

- Add his picture to the collage his peers created for him (in the previous chapter).

- Introduce him to his mentor(s) for the 90-day period and discuss what he can expect to learn.

- At some point during the first day, get him situated with his computer and show him how to get online with passwords, etc.

- Give him a building tour.

- Tell Startobe that everyone is excited about having him onboard.

- Provide an overview of the organization and the different departments.

- Discuss the organizational structure, goals, and values.

- Review his job description, outline of duties, and expectations.

- Explain how his role fits in the department and contributes to the community.

- Review his schedule and show him where they are kept and when they are updated.

- Show him his timesheet and discuss the payroll schedule.

- Discuss and clarify procedures for overtime, use of vacation and sick time, holidays, and expectations of employees on snow days. Explain any flexible work policies or procedures.

- Emphasize the commitment to care for your residents and staff. Let him know that the organization is always on the lookout for creative ways to incorporate perks and fun. Ask him to tell you one unique perk he enjoyed in a previous position and write it down.

- As you walk around, continue to introduce him to coworkers.

- Join him for lunch and share a little more about yourself. Introduce him to his lunch mates. Ask a little more about him. Don't forget to take out the Hoodsies!

- After lunch, take him into the kitchen and introduce him to the chef and kitchen staff.

- Escort him to the Human Resources department to review any lingering questions, discuss benefits, and sign or review any documents that require attention. Leave him if further discussions are necessary. Return to retrieve Startobe when that meeting is over.

Before the end of the day

The first day is a busy day for you and Startobe. Find time for the rest of these on Day 1.

- Make sure Startobe knows where the exits are located and explain emergency protocols.
- Introduce him to the Executive Director or Community Leader and allow them time to chat briefly.
- Provide water and bathroom breaks throughout the day.
- Tell him you will meet him again tomorrow morning.
- Confirm his training schedule. Even if he has been in the senior care industry, review, train, and introduce relevant computer programs, scheduling, daily expectations, resident care, etc. Review it all. Explain what the training consists of, the location, and why it is important. This will give him the basis of what is expected. *Don't overlook this.* If he tells you that he already knows the computer system, for example, don't listen to him. It is better to over-train and review a known system than to turn a new hire loose to fumble around, waste time, and feel foolish.

If time allows

- Introduce Startobe to a few positive residents—the community's ambassadors.
- If it is protocol for your community, give him key(s) and a building access card.
- Provide any additional videos or ongoing trainings. This might cause the other items listed in these steps to run longer than expected or be moved to the next day. That is perfectly fine. Ms. Keys will adjust the schedule. Try to stay on course even if things go slower than originally planned. It is better to go slowly than to rush and miss something.
- At the end of the day, take him back to your office. Ask him how he is feeling about his first day and encourage questions. Tell him you enjoyed spending time with him and hope he had an interesting day. Tell him you look forward to seeing him tomorrow at 8:00 a.m. Walk with him to retrieve his coat and personal belongings, head back to the door, shake his hand, and walk him out.

A bad first day can ruin a new job for any employee. Your role as the Engagement Coordinator is to ensure that his first impression is a great one with the promise of more to come.

Step 4

Days 2–30: Engagement Is Burning Bright

Day 2

You created great momentum on Day 1, and today you will build on that momentum.

- Wait at the door for Startobe to arrive and welcome him warmly. Take him back to your office, offer him coffee, and review the day's schedule.
- Make sure Startobe is wearing his name badge. If he forgot it, make a paper one and let him know he needs to wear it every day. Suggest he leave it at work for safekeeping.
- Ask him how he felt his first day went.

- Review yesterday's plan and adjust today's schedule to accommodate any missed steps from the day before.

- Explain how information is communicated within the organization. Email? Message boards? Newsletters?

- Encourage him to ask questions.

- Discuss the company's values and tell any stories that illustrate them.

- Set the expectations for quality care for residents. Tell him that resident care is "why we are here." We provide quality care to improve their lives for the better. Residents are our priority, and it is our privilege to serve them.

- Tell him that the culture is supportive and collaborative. Expectations include lending a helping hand to residents and employees. When he sees anyone who needs a hand, he should pitch in whenever possible.

- Tour the building again with emphasis on the locations of emergency doors, lights, alarms, fire extinguishers, and restrooms.

- Introduce him to passersby.

- Laugh easily and encourage small talk.

- Sit in on a resident activity and introduce him to residents.

- Join Startobe for lunch unless he has other plans. Buy him lunch if he forgot his.

- After lunch, Startobe will probably be anxious to get started. So, ask him, "Do you have any questions about anything we have talked about? Are you ready to jump in?" If he's ready, he will give a positive response. If he answers with a definite "yes," tell him, "That is fantastic, and I am excited for you to begin." If he is hesitant, give him time to explain. Then respond and make the necessary changes as soon as possible.

- Take him to his supervisor, and share the great news that he is ready to jump in.

Day 3–5

Startobe's supervisor will step in and join the effort in his day-to-day supervision and management of his progress. Ms. Keys will tell Startobe that she is close by and will be checking in with him at the end of the day.

The supervisor will communicate clear and high expectations for the upcoming months and how his position contributes to the community. When setting the expectations, explain the "why." Explaining

Clearly understood expectations are the foundation of a healthy and harmonious working relationship.

"why" is about justification. It is about helping him understand the bigger picture. This step is critical and will help him see how his actions and role affect the community. Clearly understood expectations are the foundation of a healthy and harmonious working relationship. It sets up Startobe for success because he will understand what a great performance should look like and why it matters. The supervisor's honesty will build trust and a strong emotional quotient of care and respect—that goes both ways.

The first few months in any new position are often a stressful time for employees as they try to fit into a new role and make good impressions. Unfortunately, most new hires are reluctant to complain or find fault with the status quo.

Create an open and comfortable connection that will engage Startobe long after the first 90 days. If he can speak freely and feel safe and respected for his thoughts and feelings, you have made the investment in his engagement.

If he can speak freely and feel safe and respected for his thoughts and feelings, you have made the investment in his engagement.

The first few days, weeks, and months present the opportune time to create a kinship. Build a positive connection every day, even if you can only squeak out a "hello" when he passes by. You want him to go home at night and tell a loved one, "I have a great boss, and she genuinely cares for me and wants me to be happy."

Research indicates that employees are more likely to leave their jobs due to a poor opinion about their boss's performance. The lack of a personal

> **For the most part, employees don't quit their jobs. They quit their bosses.**

connection means employee disengagement, so don't let this happen. For the most part, employees don't quit their jobs. They quit their bosses. Studies prove, without a doubt, the relationship the employee has with the boss is the strongest influence of all. The people who have the greatest power to keep the best employees spend the most face-to-face time with them, and therefore, have the most influence on employee retention. Take advantage of this authority and go out of your way to touch base with Startobe regularly.

Take him to his mentor and allow them to start working together.

Ms. Keys will stay involved over the course of the next 90 days in an oversight and coordination role. She will continue to check in with Startobe several times a week, observe his work and his interactions, occasionally join him for lunch, send weekly emails to say "hello," and ask him if he needs anything. She will also check in with his mentor and supervisor several times a week to learn about his progress. However, at this point, Startobe's supervisor is his go-to person, and she will be in daily communication with him. She will work with Ms. Keys, who will set up any trainings he might need or request.

Ask Startobe to check in before he leaves each day. This gives his supervisor a visual on how he is adapting and his general mood. Ask him how things are going and if he has any questions. Make sure Startobe has your email address and cell number and knows you are always available if he has any questions. Shake his hand and tell him you are happy he is on your team and that you have every confidence he is going to do wonderful things here.

Week 1

Each morning for the first few weeks, Startobe will meet up with his mentor and jump into his work schedule. The mentor will work with Startobe *and* provide time for him to work alone.

- The mentor will have lunch with Startobe each day until Startobe or the mentor has different plans. The mentor will continue to introduce him to new employees.
- Ms. Keys will join Startobe twice a week for lunch. She will take this time to ask him how he is doing and if he needs anything.
- The supervisor will check in with Startobe and his mentor in the morning and before he leaves for the day, even if it is just to say "hello."

At the End of Week 1

Invite Startobe in for a face-to-face meeting to ask him the following questions:

- How are you liking the work so far?
- Is there anything that you need that's preventing you from being more effective?
- Are there any skills you would like to learn that you feel would improve your performance?
- Whom did you meet that made a great impression?
- What makes you happy at work?

During this meeting, sit beside him at a table or side-by-side in chairs, not across from a desk. Follow this list while allowing the dialogue to take its own course, make notes, and encourage open communication. Reiterate that you are always available and want him to be happy and do well. If he communicates any concerning issues or you perceive even the hint of any issues, act upon them quickly. Do not put off to a later date an issue that is concerning. You won't get this time back. Take the opportunity to put to rest whatever issues he might have so that they are no longer a concern for him.

Week 2

Let Startobe know that he will be receiving an email with a few questions about how things are going. Ask him to respond to you by Friday afternoon before he leaves at the end of the day and to be honest with his answers. Tell him that you look forward to his reply.

- Send Startobe the email below at the end of his first week and every other week for the first 90 days. Choose words you feel are appropriate based on his position and his progress. Update and modify the message each week. Ask how things are going, mention something funny or inspirational, or acknowledge something you noticed he had done well. Below, you'll find an example of a friendly check-in.

Sample check-in email to send to Startobe

Subject: Checking in!

Hello Startobe,

How was your week? Anything exciting, interesting, or fun you can share with me? Did anyone or anything stand out to you this week? Are you feeling more settled in? Come see me if you need anything. My door is always open. I look forward to hearing from you.

Thank you,

(Startobe's supervisor)

Collect all the responses to these check-in emails from Startobe for the first 90 days.

Continue to engage with him personally through email and take advantage of this interchange to give him praise and offer feedback. Be specific in your praise and be generous whenever possible. There is nothing like knowing someone is looking out for you and that your work is noticed.

The information gathered from Startobe's responses will be very telling. It will give you a sense of how he's feeling and insight into his progress. At the end of the 90 days, you will have collected substantial information that has kept you abreast of his progress or lack thereof. This information you gathered also provides an opportunity for the manager and Startobe to talk about his learning curve and coach him where he may need guidance.

At the end of week 2—beginning of week 3

It's time for a formal review of Startobe's progress.

- Ms. Keys will conduct a meeting with Startobe's supervisor and his mentor to review and discuss Startobe's progress. This will uncover any area that may require attention. The discussion and review of this information is crucial to the engagement plan. These ongoing dialogues give you the ability to catch any issues quickly and fix them immediately before disengagement can occur.
- Make sure Startobe is part of various trainings that go beyond his position. Let him know that the community

encourages and values learning. Show him you believe he is capable of more. When you include him in these separate trainings with other managers, it will give him an idea of the expectations of other departments, help him to feel valued by the invitation, and expose him to more challenges of the community. It also networks him into the fold.

Week 3

- The supervisor will invite Startobe into her office for a weekly meeting. Work these informal meetings into his day—just to chat. This casual "check in" helps foster trust and continues the path toward full engagement. Ask his mentor to join you to share any positive feedback. However, any issues of concern should be discussed in a private, one-on-one with Startobe and his supervisor.

- Make sure these weekly check-in meetings are blocked off in your calendar, and once that time is set, don't cancel or move them around if possible. New employees want to feel important, so don't disappoint them. Continue to provide timely, on-going, spontaneous, and meaningful feedback whenever possible.

- Create a supportive network for Startobe. Introduce him to additional coworkers from different departments throughout the community who have diverse areas of expertise. Everyone has a talent, so let him see that the community acknowledges and values the different strengths each employee brings to the workplace.

- Ask Startobe what areas of additional training he feels might benefit him.

- In the first few weeks, share the goals and expectations you've outlined for him.

- Explain the performance review process, and together create written performance goals and professional development goals. Ask Startobe what his goals are and set timeframes to meet those goals. Have him write these down and give you a copy. Encourage him to push himself. Let him know you are asking him to stretch his own limits because you believe in him.

- Allow Startobe to "shadow" his supervisor at one or two high-level meetings with other colleagues to expose him to other areas of the business.

At 30 days

Ms. Keys, the supervisor, and Startobe's mentor will meet and discuss Startobe's progress and review the email responses received back from him.

Then, Ms. Keys and Startobe's supervisor will conduct a 30-day progress meeting with off-site over lunch. They will:

1. Review and discuss progress and additional training.

2. Provide him with positive feedback and obtainable goals and encourage him to ask questions and offer ideas for any department or resident care improvements.

3. Give him feedback that will help him grow.

The benefit of going off-site is that it offers a more focused discussion without distractions from the workplace.

New hires who demonstrate less than desirable results will benefit from private discussions. So many organizations *hope* to stay connected with their new staff to learn of any "warning signs" but unfortunately, unless a good onboarding program is in place, they won't see a problem until it's too late. This 30-day plan will shed light on any issues as well as on fantastic results. It will prevent you from being blindsided if Startobe comes to you to discuss a critical issue because you have been involved in his work experience since day one.

> **So many organizations *hope* to stay connected with their new staff to learn of any "warning signs," but, unfortunately, unless a good onboarding program is in place, they won't see a problem until it's too late.**

If you notice Startobe is having an issue with a coworker, lack of skill, or lack of understanding, a proven way to introduce such a sensitive subject is to open the dialogue by showing him the ROPES.

R   **Respect** for different people, experiences, opinions, levels of understanding, and risk-taking. Does he feel he might like to try something new or take a risk on ways he can improve?

O   **Openness.** Challenge yourself to consider what you are hearing; be open to other thoughts and ideas, opinions, and change. Does he feel there is a mix of different people and different perspectives, and does he see that a diversity of ideas is valued?

P   **Participation.** What you put in, you will get back. Prove you are an active observer as well as an active participant. Does he feel he can speak up and offer ideas and suggestions? Can he trust he will be heard?

E   **Education/Exploration.** We are all learners no matter where we start our journey. Does he feel ready, trained, and confident?

S   **Sensitivity** to each other and to confidentiality; i.e., what is said here, stays here. Does he feel there is mutual trust?

171

This usually results in a healthy discussion about where he is emotionally, and it touches on the points that affect most employee issues with personal relationships and professional development.

Note: The highly scheduled first-30-days plan may sound like a lot to accomplish, but creating a strong supportive and emotional connection between Startobe, his supervisor, Ms. Keys, and his mentors is critical to the engagement plan.

Think of these crucial connections like Super Glue. Each day you are placing a drop of glue between each successful interaction. From the first day, aka, the first drop of glue, you can guarantee these positive relations are going to stick and endure. The goal is for Startobe to get on board quickly and successfully—to feel immediately connected to his role, to you, and to the community. When new employees are engaged, they work hard, are happy, and are more team and goal-focused. These connections translate into lower turnover rates and higher engagement.

> **Each day you are placing a drop of glue between each successful interaction.**

Remember, you are setting the stage each day and building a world within a world for your employees. You are creating a sense of belonging and acceptance among the employees. The work environment is a large part of your employees' lives. Startobe needs to feel happy entering the building, happy to be part of something important, happy to serve residents, happy to make a difference with the knowledge that **he matters**—not unlike the comfort he feels at home.

Startobe needs to feel happy entering the building, happy to be part of something important, happy to serve residents, happy to make a difference with the knowledge that he matters—not unlike the comfort he feels at home.

Step 5

Days 31–89: The Stars Align

Startobe has been working for you for about one month. By now you have a pretty good idea of how well he is working out.

Take time to ask yourself a few questions:

- Does he appear happy?
- Is he open to feedback and discussions about his progress?
- Does he help others?
- Does he seem to enjoy talking with other employees and residents?
- What kind of attitude does he exude—positive and friendly, or negative and withdrawn?

- How is training progressing? What more can be useful to him? Check with his mentors and check with Startobe.

Take time to answer these questions. Make a note in his file about something you observe that he does well. Next time you speak with him, tell him what you saw, how much you appreciate him, and explain the kind of impact he makes on others.

Beware of the motivational vampires!

In the first 90 days, keep Startobe away from any employees who are perceived as a negative influence. Keep him away from the likes of *Saturday Night Live's* character, **You don't want him to fall in line with the wrong people who could suck the life out of Santa Claus.** "Debbie Downer." These employees are always on the lookout for people with whom they can commiserate and induct into their downward spiral. They are energy vampires. Keep him away from these employees at all costs. You want Startobe to be excited, feel inspired, and believe the work he is doing is important and that he is a part of an exceptional team. You don't want him to fall in line with the wrong people who could suck the life out of Santa Claus.

Introduce Startobe to happy, engaged employees, and pair him with them. Encourage these healthy relationships whenever possible. If you are smiling and nodding your head as you read this passage, then you agree—so be on the lookout. There is too much at stake here, so pay attention. Don't let motivational vampires, with the negativity of a meteor strike, sabotage his enthusiasm. It can happen with just a few negative words, a roll of the eyes, or a nasty comment. Keep him away from these people at all costs!

Several years ago, with great reservation, we promoted a very seasoned maintenance person. He was an excellent nail banger, but did not appear to be management material. He had been with the company for 7 years and was a steady soldier. The position of Maintenance Supervisor came up. He wanted it badly, and to be honest, we wanted him to have the position but only because we liked the guy and didn't want to lose him. We knew a lot of training was going to be necessary.

After three to four weeks of substantial basic training, he came to me smiling, and I asked him how he was doing. He said that he felt he had a new lease on life; he saw the community with fresh eyes—and he loved it. He was happy. I know we did the right thing. We gave him a chance and because we didn't want to lose him.

Many days are still filled with basic management training, which takes considerable time. The major work is trying to get him to think differently, but since he wanted the position so badly, he is learning, and he is more devoted than ever. He improves every day. He sees the faith and support we have in him, and he is engaged. From my seat, that is 90 percent success, and the rest can be taught.

Guess Who

Incorporate the following engagement game with all the immediate employees working with Startobe.

All you'll need are index cards:

The game is a fun and a phenomenal way to tighten up the team. Invite Startobe and as many team members as possible to bring their lunch. The objective of the game is for employees to learn more about one another and gain greater insight into what makes each of them tick.

Ask a shining-star employee to facilitate. Pass out small index cards and ask each staff member to write down one thing about him or herself that nobody at work knows. Tell them to submit it anonymously and not let anyone see what they wrote. Collect the cards and mix them up. Then read them out loud, one at a time, and ask the group to guess who it might be. For example, I grow pumpkins. I have a big yard, and I sow several packages of seeds in the early spring. Each fall my yard is filled with dozens of huge pumpkins, and I invite neighborhood kids over to pick them. I grow so many that I give them away to anyone and everyone I can.

When I played this game the first time, employees could not believe I did this. For some reason, they could not see me gardening. When the facilitator read my card out loud, the room went silent. When they learned that I was a pumpkin grower, it started a great conversation about what others grew, and what kind of animals they kept in their yard. It struck me how similar we all were and how much fun it was to see the human side in all of us.

One employee who had always kept to herself told us she collected snow globes. She told us that her mother, who had passed away when she was young, gave her one. It was great to learn something about her. While we were all digesting how much she had just shared with us, another employee spoke up and said she collected them too. Before the meeting was over, they had gotten together to discuss their collections.

This engagement game is all about sharing personal information and connecting on a personal level. After the game, I overheard employees talking. One of them said, "I feel like I work with really interesting people." Her friend seemed to agree. "I feel like I know everyone on a much more personal level. It was interesting," she said.

The discussions that ensue from learning about each other are priceless. Some may call this team building, but it's more than that. Sharing personal information in a safe and relaxed environment opens windows into the heart

Sharing personal information in a safe and relaxed environment opens windows into the heart and the mind. You will see employee engagement right in front of your eyes.

and the mind. You will see employee engagement right in front of your eyes.

Invite Startobe to join you for lunch to meet with a new hire from another department. Ask him to talk about the work he does and how it impacts the community. Ask them both to talk about where they are from, what work they have done, their hobbies, and other interesting tidbits. It is important to new employees to get out of the bubble of their respective departments. They need to know what personnel in different departments make up the community and how their jobs contribute to the community. It also gives them the ability to meet different employees for networking, friendships, and support. All too often, employees don't go out of their way to meet others in different areas within the community. Foster these relationships; it will allow you to see how Startobe represents his department, his attitude, and what he is saying about the work he is doing.

Utilize technology to say "hello," to remind him that training starts in a few minutes, or to wish him a nice weekend. Text has become the communication of choice, especially for the Millennials. Use it—they do!

A fantastic way to make engagement a fundamental component of the community's shared vision is to form a "Recruitment and Retention," or an R&R committee. Invite Millennials, Baby Boomers, superstars, and new stars to join the committee. Charge them with figuring out how the community can become more engaging for all demographics. This coming together of diverse groups of employees will foster team thinking and bring in creative incentives.

This committee can help the community in multiple ways. When employees are charged with business challenges, they look at these challenges with different sets of eyes. They feel responsible for the outcomes and feel part of the solution. It should be comprised of a good cross section of each department along with human resource personnel and hiring managers. The committee should meet and discuss recruitment, the 90-day guide, training, and career development. Ms. Keys should be a part of every meeting related to engagement plans and ideas.

Day 80

The 90-day engagement plan is coming to an end. At this point, you have a very good idea of how well Startobe is performing his duties. You also have met with him and his mentors many times, and you understand his level of skill and ability. Now you need to meet with him to discuss his professional development. It is time to take a pulse on the engagement plan's success.

Schedule the 90-day success meeting well in advance. Email the invitation below for this meeting. It's an example of a fun way to invite Startobe to come speak with you and talk about his experience and his continued development. On the next page, you'll find an example of a meeting invitation email.

Sample invitation email to meet with Startobe

Subject Line: 90-day Success Meeting

Dear Startobe,

Please join me for the next step in your development.

Let's discuss some things that are important to you and to us.

Is the job, team, and company what you expected?

Is there anything about your role that's still unclear?

Is there anything that you need that you don't have to do your job?

Is there something in particular that I can do to help you with your job?

What do you enjoy about the work you do?

Is there anyone who has been most helpful to you?

Please schedule a meeting with me within the next week to discuss this and anything else you'd like to talk about.

I look forward to seeing you!

Thank you,

Startobe's supervisor

Step 6

Day 90: Success—A Star Is Born

Day 90

Congratulations! You did it. You beat the odds. It is the 90th day of the engagement plan, and you have successfully engaged your new employee. Startobe has gone from a star-to-be to *Starisborn (a star is born)*! He is fully engaged and thriving. Great job, manager, and thank you, Ms. Keys. You invested a great deal of time, considerable effort and resources, and now you have a happy, engaged, shining-star employee as part of your team.

During the 90-day sit-down success meeting, don't let email, phone calls, or other employees distract you. Close your door, get out from behind your desk, and sit with Starisborn. Don't look at your phone or check your email. If you do, you'll send the message, "I'm just not that interested in you," and that is a sure and immediate morale killer.

Set aside the appropriate amount of time to discuss Starisborn's development and let others know that you are not to be interrupted during your meeting. This gives him the clear message that he is important. Other things can wait.

Here are a few discussion points:

- Ask him if he feels he has received all the training necessary to do his job up to this point.
- Find out if he is interested in developing any additional skills to perform his job.
- Ask him if he is happy and if he feels a sense of community. If yes, great; if not, ask him why not.
- Ask him to establish a few learning goals with you and write them down along with a timeframe for completion.
- Tell him that he is being relied upon to fully contribute to the success of the community, and that means he has graduated from new hire to Engagement Ambassador. Explain the importance of engagement, what it means, and how it benefits him, the team, and the work environment. Tell him it requires enthusiasm, energy, and actively supporting other employees. Ask him if he is on board with the engagement expectations.

- Tell him that meeting with you or sending you an email is a great way to communicate celebrations and concerns within the department. Ask him to reach out to you if he becomes aware of another staff member who might need help. Let him know that the best way to help a disengaged or discouraged employee is to send you a "Red Alert" message by adding "Red Alert" to the subject line and marking the email "Important." These messages are a powerful way to help employees because some won't ask for it themselves. Tell him it can be anonymous if he uses pen and paper and slips it under your door. Let him know that all managers and the leader have an open-door policy and encourage him to stop by anytime to discuss any issues whatsoever.

- Before the meeting ends, hand Starisborn a personal note card with a $90 prepaid Visa gift card. Tell him what is in the envelope and congratulate him. Tell him that you hope and expect to him to be a superstar.

After the meeting with Starisborn, reach out to Ms. Keys and the mentors with a "thank-you" and their rewards. You know them all very well, so do what it takes to give them *a bonus that means something to them*. Within reason, be prepared to give time off, additional education, or a $90 gift card. It's a small gesture but one that will be appreciated and reap rewards for you and the community.

This is how you do it: you find out what makes them tick, and then you wind their clock. Great job!

Success story: Celeste Chielle

Celeste Chielle was the epitome of a great employee. She was a smart, caring, and articulate young woman. She was very close to both grandparents and knew firsthand the emotional and physical issues of the aging. She also cared for them in their final days when the visiting home care provider was absent or running late. She spent considerable time with them when she wasn't studying or socializing with friends.

Learning and traveling were two of Celeste's passions, but she wasn't without her own share of personal issues. She had a lazy eye that became more prominent when she was intense and focused. Celeste was very aware of how she looked, and she worried that people would treat her differently because of it. Starting a new job opened that pocket of self-consciousness, and she hoped that a new boss and coworkers would be welcoming and accepting of her. She was looking forward to finding meaningful work in a professional and caring community.

Celeste had worked only six months for a senior care facility when she was promoted to Lead Resident Assistant, a position she loved. But that position was short-lived when her community was purchased by an investment group and quickly downsized, laying off about one-third of the workers. She was disappointed, but knew she would be OK. She was confident in her skills and tenacious when she wanted something.

After five weeks of job hunting, Celeste received three offers. She decided on the Homes at Stars Crossing because, during the interview, she discovered the community valued learning. They were very clear about what was expected in her role, and the woman who would be her boss had a nice, easy way that made Celeste feel comfortable.

About a week before Celeste started, she received an envelope through the mail. It was from her new company. When she opened it, she was surprised to find a card with a welcome note and several handwritten "hellos" from the Homes at Stars Crossing's staff. She also found a gift card for $40. She was elated and smiled to herself. That confirmed it; she knew she had made the right decision. Then she asked herself, "Who does this?"

A few days later, about three days before Celeste started, she received an email. It was from Ms. Keys, the woman she met during her interview. Celeste liked her and eagerly read the email. The message informed her that Ms. Keys would meet Celeste at 8:00 a.m. at the main entrance. It also let her know where to park and that lunch would be served. She was bursting at the seams with anticipation and this time, she asked herself out loud, "WHO does this?" Her roommate heard this outburst and walked into Celeste's room. "What's up?" she asked. When Celeste showed her the email, her roommate said, "Wow. No company ever did this for me. You've got it made. They like you already. Well, I guess you made the right decision choosing that job." Celeste agreed.

On the first day of Celeste's new job, she arrived just before 8:00 a.m. and easily found the employee parking section. She took her time gathering her notebook, unplugging her phone, and shutting off her car. She was happy. She felt good and already sensed a connection to the new community through the several positive communications she had received. As she *walked up to the main entrance, she saw Ms. Keys standing just inside the door. "Hello, Celeste. Welcome to Homes at Stars Crossing. Nice to see you again," she said warmly with her hand extended.*

"Hello, Ms. Keys. Thank you," Celeste replied. Before Ms. Keys uttered another word, Celeste was thanking her for the nice note and gift card she received. "I used the money to buy these new shoes," she said.

Ms. Keys looked at Celeste's shoes and with a smile, said, "Great, Celeste—looks like you put it to good use. It was my pleasure." They walked down the hall, smiling at passersby, and talking about that day's schedule.

After a full but interesting day, which included meeting new co-workers, residents, and learning her way around the building, Celeste drove home. When she arrived, her roommate was in the kitchen making dinner. "Well, how did it go?" she asked.

With a big smile, Celeste looked at her roommate and said, "They had me at hello."

Conclusion

Senior living is a highly personal and hands-on service business. Most of the encounters occur between a single staff member and a resident or family member. The quality of that experience, as perceived by the residents and their families, is key to everything you do. If your employee is engaged, interactions will go well. In the senior care industry, high-quality service is not a part-time business: it is an everyday expectation and the demands are great. It is essential that employees be engaged in the work they do and rewarded for their engagement.

During the first 90 days, new employees are highly vulnerable. Take advantage of this opportunity and shower them with all your best practices. Show your heart. Be part of their journey. This vulnerability works in your favor. This is the time to show them how great it will be to work with you, and let them know they can expect more to come. The 90-day window is open to many first impressions, so impress the heck out of them. It can also feel like a honeymoon period of sorts, and new hires are expecting to feel excited and cared for as they provide value to the organization. Don't let them down. Give them feedback, training, and check in often. For a new employee, the first 90 days can feel like forever if they haven't heard from you, seen you, had face-to-face conversations, or received necessary training or feedback.

Your job in the first 90 days is to find out what makes your employees tick and then provide them with the opportunities, training, and tools to bring that to life. A learning community is an

All the learning and creativity in the world are worthless if you don't implement what is learned—through *action*.

engaged community, but all the learning and creativity in the world are worthless if you don't implement what is learned—through *action*. Without action, the other ingredients in this recipe don't amount to anything. Sometimes organizations get so caught up in the learning process that they don't actually use the knowledge they gained. To implement the 90-day guide requires persistence and a commitment to achieve the goals set forth.

The biggest challenge in any employee engagement plan for most communities is tracking each employee to find out how she or he is feeling about the work and the team. But you won't have this problem because you have the steps necessary to track those critical first 90 days.

Tracking is imperative because you need to be able to follow employees closely to understand where each of them stands in their professional development, identify any issues, and then act quickly. Regular check-ins, informal meetings, and trainings are a powerful and effective way to show employees that the organization is committed to their happiness and success.

However, that is a tall order in a busy community, which is why a dedicated Engagement Coordinator is at the heart of this guide and holds the keys to a successful engagement plan. The Engagement Coordinator must devote time to track progress, and move around the different departments to regularly "check in" and take the pulse of new employees' development, energy levels, and moods to identify any issues before a new employee shows signs of disengagement.

Any leader or manager will tell you that it is easier to engage on a regular basis than to try to reverse the disengagement. So many

It is easier to engage on a regular basis than to try to reverse the disengagement.

organizations *hope* to stay connected with their new staff members to discover any warning signs; unfortunately, unless a good onboarding program is in place with a key person tracking the new employees, they won't see a problem until it's too late.

The bottom line is this: Engagement won't happen by chance, and it's not unlike growing pumpkins. The seeds need to soak overnight even before they hit the dirt. They have to feel their journey has begun. They need to be carefully planted together but with enough space between them to allow for growth, watered with praise, welcomed with warmth, and trained to grow strong. As they grow, they need support to feel strong and vital, all the while encircled within the framework of others. It takes a strategic approach and a nurturing eye for roots to take hold for a long and healthy harvest. Throwing a few seeds on the dirt doesn't grow pumpkins, and it doesn't create a harvest of engagement.

It really all comes down to what motivates and inspires your employees. In the first 90 days, listen to what excites them, keep an ongoing dialogue with them, and use informal discussions while checking in with them to say "hello." You will gain insight into the kinds of things that motivate each individual staff member, and you'll be engaging with them on a personal level. Employees are as different as stars in the universe; don't make any assumptions. If you want to know what makes *your* employees tick, just ask.

Beyond the first 90 days

By following the steps in this book, you will accomplish what many community leaders have not been able to do. You will engage your new employees, allowing you to hang on to your stars. However, it is vital to continue to engage your employees to keep them happy and effectively contributing to your organization.

In my next book, I will show you exactly how to engage your employees beyond the first 90 days. The fact is you need to do this. You owe it to your employees to continue to provide them with support, feedback, and learning opportunities. But a fundamental reason to keep your stars engaged is to *save a fortune in recruiting and hiring costs* by building a sustainable community of engaged employees. Don't budget for failure; plan for success.

Meanwhile, you have learned the traits necessary to communicate effectively and the steps to take to show your employees how important they are to your organization. Apply what you have learned so far. Create a home away from home and an engaging environment where your employees feel a part of something exciting and important. And that mission, my friend, is possible. Remember, engagement is like learning; it is a process, not a result. Don't stop engaging, don't stop learning, and never give up. Studies show that most people give up right before attaining success. Be consistent in your engagement practices and practice them constantly. Action is the wheel of success. Employees are just a different kind of customer. Without them, where would you be?

Appendix

Exit Interviews

If an employee leaves during the first 90-day engagement plan, which is highly unlikely if you follow the steps in this book, take every opportunity to meet with him or her before he or she leaves, and make it count. Most organizations require managers to perform an exit interview; however, in researching this subject, they just don't get done.

Most often when employees tell you they are leaving, they tell you why. Many managers don't take the time to press further and learn why and when they disengaged. They don't ask what is working and what isn't. There is valuable information to be gained about how departing employees perceive their roles, their departments, and the organizations.

This information is invaluable. It allows you the chance to make improvements that result in greater employee engagement.

Keep in mind that the exit interview has a greater chance of success when conducted by a second or third manager removed. It will produce more honest feedback. Ensure a second person is present to take notes as well as for legal purposes. Four ears hear better than two.

In smaller communities, exit interviews can be uncomfortable, given the familiarity between management and employees. An exit interview is not for the weak of heart. It might take a bit of diplomacy, emotional intelligence, or a combination of both to redirect and calm the departing employee if things get negative or even nasty. It can be challenging to stay the course and remain objective, for example, while listening to stories about employees and their not-so-stellar behaviors. But it is not something that should cause you stress. Look at it as continuing education, and know that you will learn something you don't already know that could make a big impact on the community—because it's true.

Conducting an exit interview also sends the message to departing employees that the company cares about their opinions. It might seem fruitless to gain points with a departing (and possibly unhappy) employee, but nothing could be further from the truth. That feedback will tell you where the community came up short. One of a company's key goals is employee retention; therefore, it is critical to discover what made an employee unhappy enough to want to leave. In addition to mining vital information, the interview can also reduce your exposure to discrimination, harassment, and employment claims if the employee brings this up as part of the discussion. Furthermore, you have the opportunity to leave the employee with a better lasting impression than he or she would otherwise have.

Top questions companies use to gain intelligence from departing employees

1. Instead of asking why they are leaving their current position, ask why they started looking.
2. Did we provide you with what you needed to do your job well?
3. How do you feel things went here?
4. Where did we go wrong?
5. Do you have suggestions for improvements?
6. What could your manager have done differently?
7. What is your new employer giving you that you did not get from us?
8. What did you like most about your job?
9. What did you dislike most about your job?
10. What was the biggest factor that led you to accept this new job or caused you to want to leave?
11. What skills and qualifications do you think we need to look for in your replacement?
12. How does your new job fulfill your career goals?
13. What are the top three things you will remember?
14. Would you like us to stay in touch to let you know about future opportunities?

When the interview is over, thank them, wish them well, and walk them out. Leave on the best possible terms. You never know if this person will be asked about your facility. Bad news and poor reputations travel faster than the flu. Stay positive and say good-bye as eloquently and respectfully as possible. Make a copy of their responses for their manager, Ms. Keys, and the leader. Place it in the employee's file. Take the responses to the next meeting and discuss the information with the team.

Be careful to omit any information that might prove hurtful or damaging to a named employee (which could place the facility in legal jeopardy).

Ask Ms. Keys to start a spreadsheet to track the questions and employees' answers. Periodically compare responses and identify any commonalities that might uncover blind spots in your organization. This information is worth its weight in gold. Keep it accessible, identify areas you can change and improve on, and then do it. Keep your learning machines in tip-top shape. They are your best weapon to hang on to your stars.

Let's Connect

Note from the Author

Dear Reader,

I hope you've enjoyed *Hang on to Your Stars*. I wrote it to help you stamp out chronic turnover and save you a bundle in hiring costs while creating happy and engaged employees. There is so much to building sustainable engaged communities and here's how I can help you to learn more:

 Speaking engagements

1. Leadership strategies to create sustainable communities of engaged workers.

2. Management discussion groups on engagement strategies and best practices.

 Consulting

3. "Community Engagement Assessments" of your community's first 90-day engagement practices, provide recommendations, and implement engagement solutions.

4. "Employee Engagement Assessments" of your employees, past and present to determine why you are experiencing high turnover, make recommendations and implement steps to engage employee today.

Visit my website at www.hangontoyourstars.com. Sign up for my newsletter as well as for announcements on my speaking engagements and the release of my upcoming book, *Hang on to Your Stars: Volume 2, Beyond the First 90 Days.*

Reach out to me. I want to help you to hang onto *your* stars.

Thank you
Doreen A. Lang
Email: doreen@hangontoyourstars.com

P.S. If you've enjoyed this book and find its information helpful, please write a review at www.amazon.com. I can't wait to hear from you!

References

Age Wave. (2016). http://www.agewave.com.

American Immigration Council. (February 14, 2012). The Future of a Generation: How New Americans Will Help Support Retiring Baby Boomers. Retrieved from https://www.americanimmigrationcouncil.org/research/future-generation-how-new-americans-will-help-support-retiring-baby-boomers.

American Psychological Association. (2014, April 23). Employee distrust is pervasive in U.S. workforce. Retrieved from http://www.apa.org/news/press/releases/2014/04/employee-distrust.

Billington, D. (1988, 2000) Ego development and adult education (Doctoral Dissertation, the Fielding Institute).

Retrieved from Dissertation Abstracts International, 49 (p. 7). (University Microfilms No. 88-16, p. 275).

Brookfield, S. (1986). Understanding and facilitating adult learning. San Francisco: Jossey-Bass.

Bureau of Labor Statistics. (August 4, 2017). The employment situation—July 2017. Retrieved from https://www.bls.gov/news.release/pdf/empsit.pdf.

Cantor, J. (1992). Delivering instruction to adult learners. Toronto: Wall & Emerson.

Cirillo, A. (2017, February 26). The advantages of career ladders. Verywell. Retrieved from https://www.verywell.com/the-advantages-of-career-ladders-197844.

Collins. J. (2001). Good to great: Why some companies make the leap… and others don't. New York: HarperBusiness.

Compdata Surveys/Consulting. (August 25, 2016). 2016 Total Turnover Rates by State. Retrieved from http://www.compensationforce.com/2017/04/2016-turnover-rates-by-industry.html.

Dunn, R., & Dunn, K. (1987). Understanding learning styles and the need or individual diagnosis and prescription. Columbia, CT: The Learner's Dimension.

Employee engagement. (n.d.). In Business Dictionary. Retrieved from http://www.businessdictionary.com/definition/employee-engagement.html.

Employee Engagement in Senior Care. (2017). A Whitepaper from OnShift. The Key to Success in 2017.

Engelbert, C. (2017, March 21). Job-stealing robots? Millennials see hope, fear in automation. LinkedIn. Retrieved from https://www.linkedin.com/pulse/job-stealing-robots-millennials-see-hope-fear-cathy-engelbert.

Felder, R. (1996, December). Matters of Style. ASEE Prism, 6(4), 18–23.

Flemming, D., & Mills, C. (1992). Not another inventory, rather a catalyst for reflection. New York: Balsam Books Inc.

Gagne, R. (1985). The conditions of learning and theory of instruction (4th ed.). Ft. Worth, TX: Holt, Rinehart, and Winston.

Gallup News. (2106). How Millennials Want to Work and Live. Retrieved from http://news.gallup.com/reports/189830/e.aspx.

Gallup News. Few Millennials are Engaged at Work. Retrieved from http://news.gallup.com/businessjournal/195209/few-millennials-engaged-work.aspx.

Gallup Workplace. Drive Employee Engagement. Retrieved from http://workplace.gallup.com/215921/optimize-employee-engagement.aspx.

Gardner, H. (1993). Multiple intelligences: The theory in practice. New York: Basic Books Inc.

Garvin, D. (2000). Learning in action: A guide to putting the learning organization to work. Boston: Harvard Business School Press.

Graham, A. (2014, May 5). 10 new powerful senior living statistics. LeadingAge. Retrieved from http://www.leadingage.org/corporatepartners/10-new-powerful-senior-living-stats.

Harvard Business Review. (2013). The impact of employee engagement on performance. A Report by Harvard Business Review Analytic Services. Harvard Business School Publishing. Retrieved from https://hbr.org/resources/pdfs/comm/achievers/hbr_achievers_report_sep13.pdf.

Hersey, P., & Blanchard, K. (1977). Management of organizational behavior: Utilizing human resources. Englewood Cliffs, NJ: Prentice-Hall.

Hersey, P., & Keilty, J. W. (1980). Interaction influence. San Francisco: Jossey-Bass.

Hiemstra, R. (1991). Creating environments for effective adult learning. San Francisco: Jossey-Bass.

Honold, L. (2000). Developing employees who love to learn. Palo Alto, CA: Davies-Black Publishing.

Imel, S. (1994). Guidelines for working with adult learners. Retrieved October 26, 2001 from ERIC database (ED377313) http://ericir.syr.edu.

Kaye, B., & Jordan-Evans, S. (2014). Love'em or lose'em: Getting good people to stay. San Francisco: Berrett-Koehler Publishers.

Kelleher, B. (2010). Louder than words: Ten employee engagement steps that drive results. Portland, OR: BLKB Publishing.

Knowles, M. (1984). Andragogy in action: Applying modern principles of adult learning. San Francisco: Jossey-Bass.

Kolb, D. (1984). Experiential learning: Experience as the source of learning and development. Upper Saddle River, NJ: Prentice-Hall.

Krames, J. (2003). What the best CEOs know. New York: McGraw-Hill.

Livingston, G. (2015, May 5). Family size among mothers. Pew Research Center. Retrieved from http://www.pewsocialtrends.org/2015/05/07/family-size-among-mothers/.

Menkes, J. (2006). Executive intelligence: What all great leaders have. New York: HarperCollins.

Merhar, C. (2016, February 4). Employee retention – The real cost of losing an employee. Retrieved from https://www.zanebenefits.com/blog/bid/312123/employee-retention-the-real-cost-of-losing-an-employee.

Merriam, S., & Caffarella, R. (1984). Learning in adulthood: A comprehensive guide. San Francisco: Jossey-Bass.

Modern Workforce. (January 19, 2017). The Scary Truth About Millennials Being Disengaged At Work. Retrieved from https://www.geteverwise.com/talent-development/the-scary-truth-about-millennials-being-disengaged-at-work/.

Peters, T. (2010). The little big things: 163 ways to pursue excellence. New York: HarperCollins.

Pratt, D. (1992) Chinese conceptions of learning and teaching: A Westerner's attempt at understanding. International Journal of Lifelong Education, 11(4), 301–320.

Rogers, J. (1989). Adults learning (3rd ed.). Philadelphia, PA: Open University Press.

Ryback, D. (1998). Putting emotional intelligence to work: Successful leadership is more than IQ. Boston: Butterworth-Heinemann.

Schein, E. (1992). Organizational culture and leadership. San Francisco: Jossey-Bass.

Senge, P. (1990). The fifth discipline: The art and practice of the learning organization. London: Random House.

Senge, P., Camron-McCabe, N., Lucas, T., Smith, B., Dutton, J., & Kleiner, A. (2000). Schools that learn. A fifth discipline field book for educators, parents, and everyone who cares about education. New York: Doubleday/Currency.

Senge, P., Kleiner, A., Roberts, C., Ross, R., Roth, G., & Smith, B. (1990). The dance of change: The challenges of sustaining momentum in learning organizations. New York: Doubleday/Currency.

Sheehy, G. (1976). Passages: Predictable crises of adult life. New York: Dutton.

Stack, F. (1992). The great game of business. New York: Currency Doubleday.

Variety Games Inc. (2013). Make your own printable crossword puzzles. Retrieved from https://www.puzzle-maker.com/crossword_Entry.cgi.

Vella, J. (1994). Learning to listen. Learning to teach: The power of dialogue in educating adults. San Francisco: Jossey-Bass.

About The Author
Doreen A. Lang

Author, Speaker, and Consultant

Doreen Lang wrote *Hang on to Your Stars, The First 90 Days: Step-by-Step Employee Engagement Solution for the Senior Living Community* to help leaders and managers in senior living communities achieve highly profitable communities through employee engagement. Her first book provides a money-saving, step-by-step solution for retaining employees during the critical first 90 days based on her 25 years of experience in the field.

Her second book, due for publication in 2018 will show you how to *Hang on to Your Stars, Beyond the First 90 Days*. This second volume will help you learn the rules of engagement, so you can hang on to your stars far beyond the critical first 90 days. Combined, these two books provide all you need to engage your staff from day one and keep them committed to your community all the while—shining brightly.

Doreen is passionate about creating successful communities through employee engagement and specializes in inspiring leaders and managers to build harmonious work environments. She is currently the General Manager of a 55+ community where she turned around a dysfunctional and ineffective team, implementing practices she designed and delivered. Previously, she was Senior Operations Manager of an independent, assisted living, and memory care community where she played a fundamental role in orientation, training, and development by implementing her own tried-and-true practices to develop and retain new employees. Doreen has enjoyed 100 percent staff retention in every position she has held. She practices what she preaches!

Widely published in her field, Doreen has contributed business articles on topics of employee retention and leadership strategies for the *Mass High Tech* newspaper, *The Boston Globe*, and Regional newspapers.

In the past, Doreen has taught Marketing Fundamentals and Entrepreneurship at Bentley University and Entrepreneurial Management and Managerial Leadership and Communications at Bay State College.

Doreen earned her Master's in Management with a concentration in organizational development from Cambridge College, and a bachelor's degree in Education from UMass Boston, where she received the '*Excellence in Teaching Award*'. She began the Ph.D. program in Educational Leadership at Southeastern University.

In Doreen's workshops and presentations, her passion for inspiring leaders on successfully retaining employees through engagement stands out. She provides a variety of popular and sought-after inspirational talks and workshops, including "Hang on to Your Stars," "The First 90 Days is Key," and "Inspiring Leaders" as well as custom workshops. Her goal is to inspire leaders, executive directors, department managers, and human resources professionals to create engaged communities where staff want to work and residents want to live. Reach out to her to help you become a CEO, a Chief Engagement Officer and lead your community to success!

Email: doreen@hangontoyourstars.com

Made in the USA
Middletown, DE
30 January 2018